The Magic of the Forest

in Cross Stitch and Watercolour

The Magic of the Forest

in Cross Stitch and Watercolour

Jan Woodman

The Watermark Press

Published by The Watermark Press, Sydney, 2002
Text, illustrations, cross stitch embroideries and pattern charts copyright © Jakegi Designs
2002

Designer: Jan Woodman
Scans: Command E
Printed and bound in Singapore by Imago Productions

National Library of Australia Cataloguing-in-Publication Data

Woodman, Jan.
Magic of the forest : in cross stitch and watercolour.
ISBN 0 9 492 84 599.

Dedicated to my parents who taught me to love our wildflowers from a very early age,
to our children, Stuart and Susan and their partners Sue and Brian
and to our wonderful grandchildren,
Timothy, Ashlea, Kirsty and Jessica.

ACKNOWLEDGEMENTS

Firstly I would like to thank my husband, Keith, who has helped and supported me with every aspect of this book. His confidence and assistance, particularly in transferring my roughly drawn charts into beautiful computerised ones, has been invaluable.

Thanks to Sophie Bruns Kemperman for her hours of patient stitching of many of the cross stitch embroideries.

Thank you to Dianna and Stany de Hauteclocque of Stadia Handcrafts, for agreeing to let me include my designs of the 'Superb Blue Wren' and the 'New Holland Honeyeater'; to friends and clients who have kindly allowed me to reproduce their paintings, and to everyone else who has helped make it possible to produce this book.

A special thank you to Sally Milner for her help and guidance.

Contents

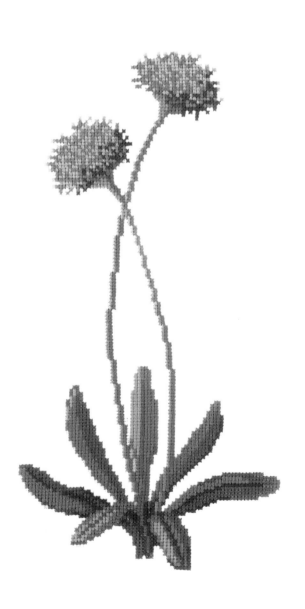

Wildflowers

There is something very special about wildflowers, particularly when seen growing in their natural environment. Many species are now extinct and many more becoming endangered, mainly due to the ever-decreasing areas of natural vegetation.

I suppose my love of wildflowers and native orchids began at a very early age. My parents had a great love of the outback and the bush and many weekends were spent bushwalking and hunting for orchids. My Father was an avid photographer and my Mother was a landscape artist who delighted in painting the beauty of the outback.

It was not until Keith and I and our two children moved to live in the country during the late 1970s that I became really interested in wildflowers again. Our property had many areas of natural forest, with many other areas in close proximity and I became fascinated in watching the different species of flowers and orchids develop from the tiniest shoot or leaf through to their flowering each spring.

The fascination became an obsession to record the flowers and so I began drawing lessons and started to draw the flowers using a simple stipple technique. I then adapted these drawings to petitpoint and surface embroidery

In the mid 1980s I began studying flower painting using the medium of pure watercolour and was also given the chance to study plants and their structure under the tutelage of botanists at the State Herbarium of South Australia in the Botanic Gardens.

My love developed for painting groups of the smaller herbaceous plants and ground orchids, growing amongst the associated mosses, ferns, toadstools and fungi and surrounded with the debri and leaf litter of the forest floor.

As I also love embroidery, it has been a natural progression for me to adapt my paintings into designs for cross stitch.

Keith and I now live in the beautiful coastal town of Stansbury on Yorke Peninsula, South Australia, overlooking the bay and with close access to many areas of scrub and conservation parks.

Whenever we get the chance we take off in our caravan and go further afield, combining our love of fishing with wildflower hunting.

The 'magic' of the forest and the bush will never cease to excite me.

Finger Flower

Finger Flower *(Cheiranthera alternifolia)*

A very attractive small shrub with graceful branches
that are crowded with narrow leaves and support
beautiful violet or blue flowers. The five stamens
and their large orange-yellow anthers all turn to
one side of the pistil and look like five fingers on a
hand, hence the common name of 'Finger Flower'.

**Key for DMC
stranded cotton:**

✕	209
L	210
I	211
▲	333
○	340
⅂	341
◤	433
∩	436
●	444
■	791
⌐	912
◢	3345
＼	3347

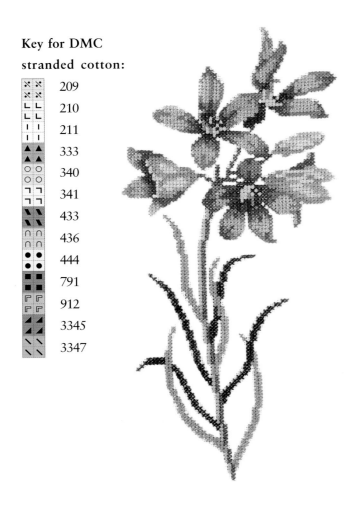

Stitch Count: 60 across
129 down

Flannel Flower

Flannel Flower *(Actinotus helianthi)*

An erect plant with soft grey-green leaves that is easily recognised by its spreading velvet bracts that look like petals. The centre of the flower within these bracts consists of many tiny flowers, without petals and with very small sepals.

Key for DMC stranded cotton:

I I / I I	ecru
I I / I I	320
I I / I I	368
← ← / ← ←	420
○○ / ○○	612
– – / – –	734
□□ / □□	895
■■ / ■■	935
▲▲ / ▲▲	3012
◆◆ / ◆◆	3013
×× / ××	

Stitch Count: 54 across
128 down

Painting opposite page: Flannel Flower and Wiry Bauera

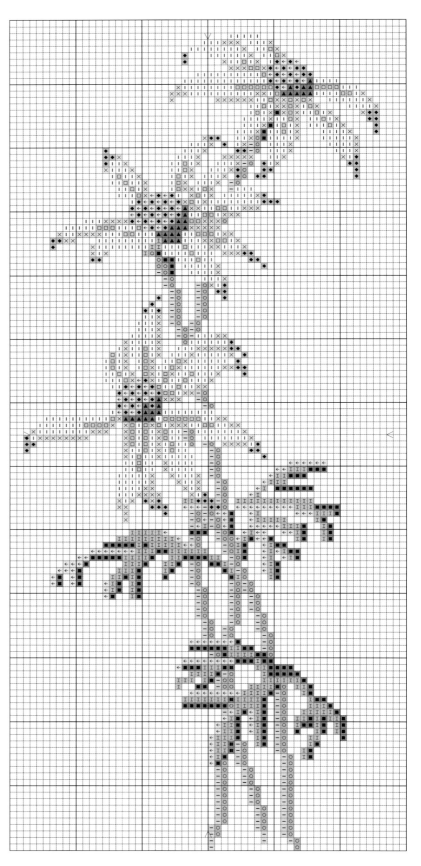

Wiry Bauera

Wiry Bauera *(Bauera rubioides)*
A scrambling bushy shrub with pretty pink and white flowers. This plant is widespread in damp areas of heaths and forests and flowers most of the year.

The three dimensional look of the flowers was enhanced by working the sepals with only one strand of DMC 780.

Key for DMC stranded cotton:

● ●	444
╱ ╱	445
∨ ∨	471
I I	780
▲ ▲	937
+ +	3685
○ ○	3687
⌐ ⌐	3689

Stitch Count: 53 across

69 down

Downy Mintbush

Downy Mintbush *(Prostanthera behriana)*

A medium upright or straggling shrub with soft hairy stems. The flowers are light purple or lilac and have reddish dots in the throat. The light green leaves are aromatic when crushed.

Stitch Count: 32 across
66 down

Key for DMC stranded cotton:

T T / T T	208
\ \ / \ \	209
I I / I I	211
▲ ▲ / ▲ ▲	327
■ ■ / ■ ■	550
N N / N N	553
∞ ∞ / ∞ ∞	554
U U / U U	725
> > / > >	841
F F / F F	987
– – / – –	989
X X / X X	3740

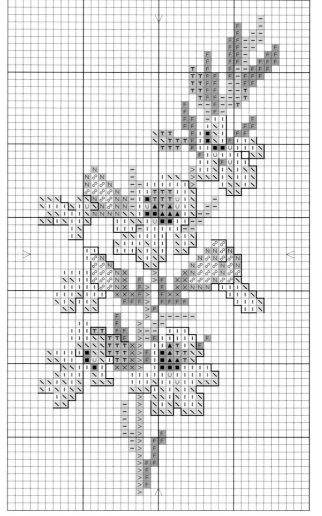

Backstitch around petal edges as shown with one strand of DMC 553.
Work **French knots** with one strand of DMC 676 for the stamens.

Lotus Waterlily

Lotus Waterlily *(Nelumbo nucifera)*
The Lotus Waterlily or Sacred Lotus is an aquatic perennial herb that grows in the waterways of tropical areas. The large leaves are orbicular on long, thick stalks usually well above the surface. The solitary flowers are red to pink, yellow or white, with numerous yellow stamens.

The yellow stamens of this lily would also be ideal for working in surface stitchery. Try working French knots using two strands of DMC 3822 and 3820 with the addition of a few small yellow beads.

Key for DMC stranded cotton:

U U / U U	ecru
/ / / /	309
■ ■ / ■ ■	310
J J / J J	335
O O / O O	420
6 6 / 6 6	470
V V / V V	471
− − / − −	472
□ □ / □ □	734
• • / • •	738
I I / I I	746
◆ ◆ / ◆ ◆	783
e e / e e	899
× × / × ×	927

Z Z / Z Z	931
= = / = =	932
L L / L L	3011
● ● / ● ●	3021
◢ ◢ / ◢ ◢	3345
H H / H H	3346
\ \ / \ \	3347
✓ ✓ / ✓ ✓	3348
▼ ▼ / ▼ ▼	3362
→ → / → →	3716
▲ ▲ / ▲ ▲	3721
T T / T T	3821
∕ ∕ / ∕ ∕	3822

(Use only one strand of DMC 932 for the water)

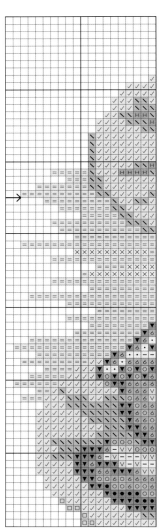

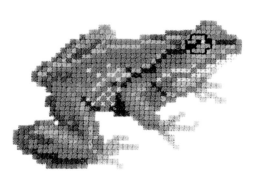

Stitch Count: 119 across

87 down

Blue Pincushion

Blue Pincushion *(Brunonia australis)*

An attractive perennial herb with large basal leaves. Flowers are usually a deep sky-blue, occasionally pale blue or white. The large flower heads on long leafless stems are made up of dense masses of tiny flowers.

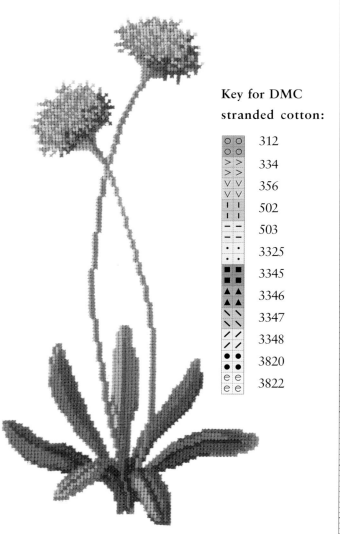

Key for DMC stranded cotton:

○ ○ / ○ ○	312
> > / > >	334
∨ ∨ / ∨ ∨	356
I I / I I	502
— — / — —	503
· · / · ·	3325
■ ■ / ■ ■	3345
▲ ▲ / ▲ ▲	3346
\ \ / \ \	3347
/ / / / /	3348
● ● / ● ●	3820
e e / e e	3822

Stitch Count: 76 across
156 down

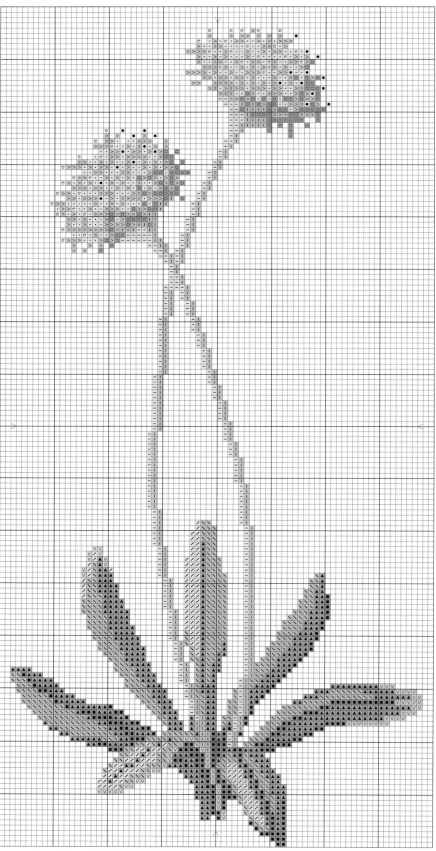

19

Silver-leaved Daisy

Silver-leaved Daisy *(Olearia pannosa)*

A rather straggly but pretty shrub that is quite rare. Beautiful large white or white and pink-tipped flowers look startling against the large dark green mature leaves. The younger leaves and buds have a silvery-white appearance, hence the common name 'Silver-leaved Daisy'.

The white daisies above were embroidered on a blue linen background. Alter the thread and background colours to suit your own colour schemes. The pink daisy on the left was embroidered on an off-white linen background and the 'petals' worked with DMC thread colours 3689, 3688 and 3687. French knots were then added to further embellish the daisy centre. Note that this single daisy taken from a section of the chart on the right has been horizontally reversed. One of the simplest ways of reversing a design is to photocopy the chart onto tracing paper, and then simply work from the reverse side of the tracing paper.

Painting on previous page:

Soft Millotia *(Millotia tenuifolia)*, Milkmaids *(Burchardia umbellata)*, Blue Pincushion *(Brunonia australis)*, Tall Bluebell *(Wahlenbergia stricta)*, King Spider Orchid *(Caladenia tentaculata)*, Common Riceflower *(Pimelea humilis)* and Native Primrose *(Goodenia blackiana)*.

Key for DMC cotton:

· · / · ·	white
O O / O O	316
◆ ◆ / ◆ ◆	319
I I / I I	320
← ← / ← ←	368
● ● / ● ●	444
╱ ╱ / ╱ ╱	445
∧ ∧ / ∧ ∧	504
+ + / + +	778
⊞ ⊞ / ⊞ ⊞	780
R R / R R	783
< < / < <	3042
■ ■ / ■ ■	3345
▲ ▲ / ▲ ▲	3346
╲ ╲ / ╲ ╲	3347

Stitch Count:

88 across

126 down

Waratah Chart 2

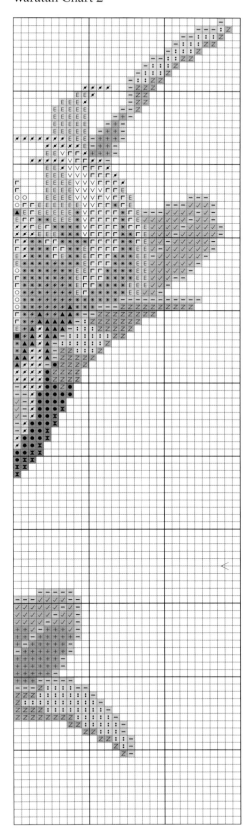

Waratah

Waratah *(Telopea speciosissima)*

These beautiful Waratahs with their brilliant red and yellow bracts were given to me to paint by a friend from her magnificent native garden.

This native garden was planted in 1930 by my friend's grandfather, William Burdett, and is now Heritage listed.

Waratah Chart 3

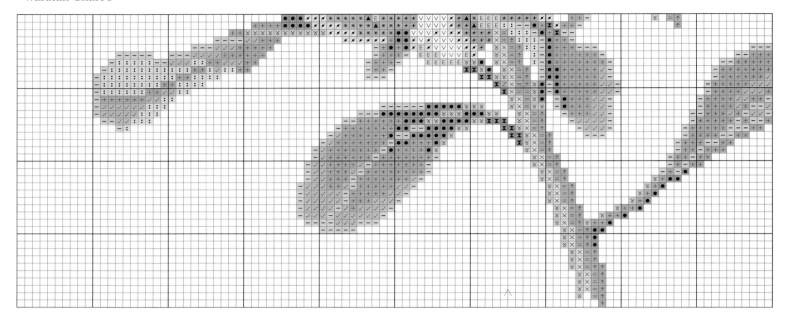

Stitch Count: 127 across
150 down

Waratah Chart 4

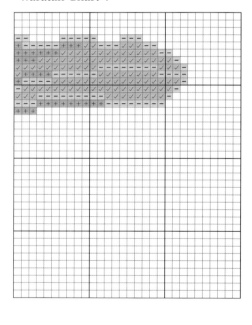

Key for DMC stranded cotton:

✳ ✳	309	
⌀ ⌀	371	
U U	372	
Z Z	470	
∴ ∴	471	
= =	610	
✕ ✕	612	
– –	734	
⌐ ⌐	760	
○ ○	761	
▲ ▲	814	

⚡ ⚡	816
✗ ✗	890
✦ ✦	977
● ●	3345
+ +	3346
✓ ✓	3347
◼ ◼	3371
E E	3712
↑ ↑	3781
v v	3822
I I	3823

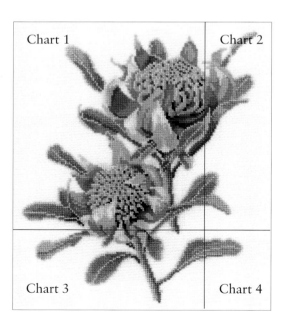

Chart 1   Chart 2

Chart 3   Chart 4

The chart for the Waratah has been split up into four sections as shown here.

24

Jan Woodman 1997

Daisy, Eyebright & Logania

Fringed Daisy *(Olearia ciliata)*—a dwarf shrub with bright green narrow leaves and purple flowers.

Eyebright *(Euphrasia collina)*—a very pretty small herb with pale pink or white petals, now very rare.

Coast Logania *(Logania crassifolia)*—a low shrub with white flowers found on coastal dunes and cliffs.

Key for DMC stranded cotton:

white	778
316	780
327	783
470	937
471	987
472	988
553	3052
554	3778
612	
676	
743	

Stitch Count: 59 across
89 down

Wildflower Bouquets

Wildflower Bouquet 1

Flannel Flower *(Actinotus helianthi)*
Waratah *(Telopea speciosissima)*
Sturt's Desert Rose *(Gossypium sturtianum)*
Common Heath *(Epacris impressa)*
Golden Wattle *(Acacia pycnantha)*
Finger Flower *(Cheiranthera alternifolia)*
Royal Bluebell *(Wahlenbergia gloriosa)*

Wildflower Bouquet 2

Lilac Hibiscus *(Alogyne huegelii)*
Australian Hollyhock *(Lavatera plebeia)*
Pink-eyed Susan *(Tetratheca pilosa)*
Bearded Heath *(Leucopogon virgatus)*
Wiry Bauera *(Bauera rubioides)*
Guinea Flower *(Hibbertia sp)*
Lavender Grevillea *(Grevillea lavandulacea)*

These two wildflower bouquets are similar in size and have been designed for cross-stitch and tapestry.
A key for both DMC stranded cotton and DMC tapestry wool is included.
Their size makes them ideal for embroidering as a pair of cushions, seat covers, or framed pictures.

Wildflower Bouquet 1

Wildflower Bouquet Chart 1

Wildflower Bouquet Chart 2

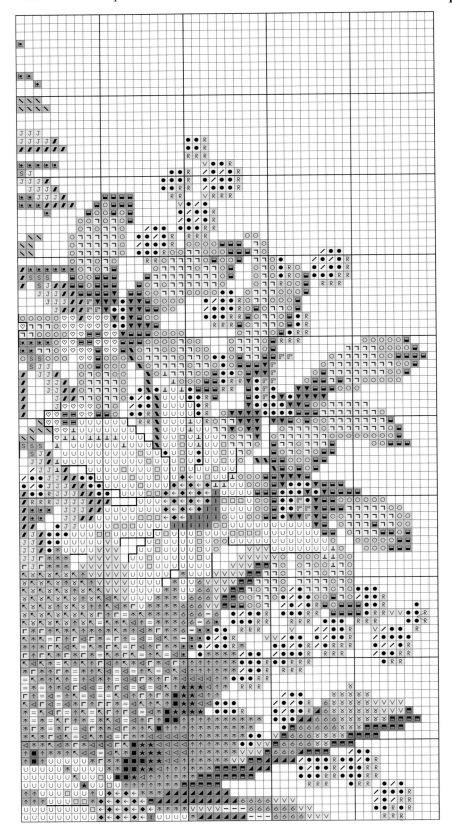

Key for DMC stranded cotton & tapestry wool:

	cotton	wool		cotton	wool
✗✗	209	7243	==	754	7192
LL	210	7241	✗✗	782	7782
∷∷	211	7241	RR	783	7782
↑↑	304	7544	▼▼	791	7307
//	309	7758	⊗⊗	809	7302
II	320	7542	◁◁	815	7110
⊟⊟	333	7306	♡♡	818	7200
○○	340	7304	✗✗	825	7304
⅂⅂	341	7302	>>	841	7524
↖↖	350	7759	⊟⊟	895	7541
⌐⌐	352	7760	JJ	899	7205
SS	355	7758	★★	902	7375
←←	368	7954	⌐⌐	912	7386
↓↓	420	7541	II	935	7398
◥◥	433	7416	◆◆	3012	7404
●●	444	7725	⊥⊥	3013	7402
∕∕	445	7078	ee	3326	7202
66	470	7427	◣◣	3345	7428
VV	471	7376	▨▨	3346	7386
−−	472	7373	\\	3347	7384
⋈⋈	500	7389	⊟⊟	3350	7208
∥∥	612	7404	■■	3371	7535
⌗⌗	666	7666	ZZ	3687	7205
⋈⋈	729	7361	⊡⊡	3688	7202
□□	734	7361	⅗⅗	3689	7200
<<	743	7725	UU	ecru	ecru

Backstitching:

Common Heath - backstitch around the pale pink petals using one strand of DMC 899
Flannel Flower - backstitch as shown on the lower 'petals' using one strand of DMC 3012

Stitch Count: 138 across
147 down

Wildflower Bouquet Chart 3

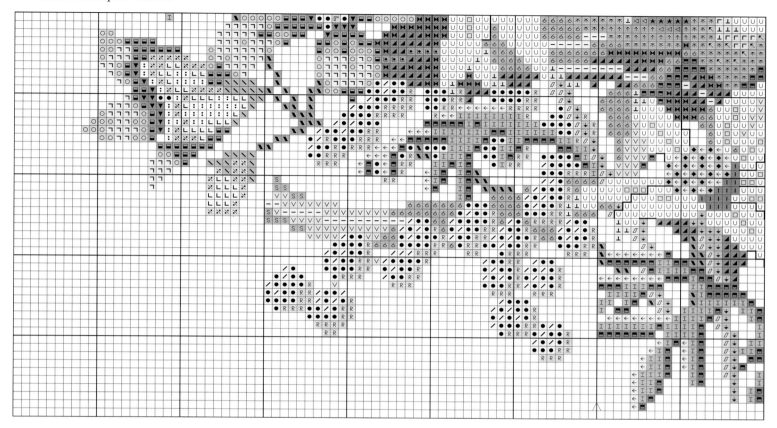

Wildflower Bouquet Chart 4

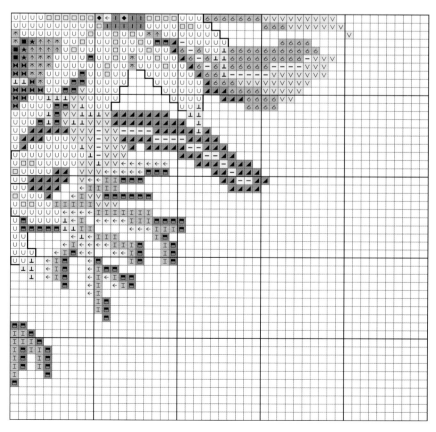

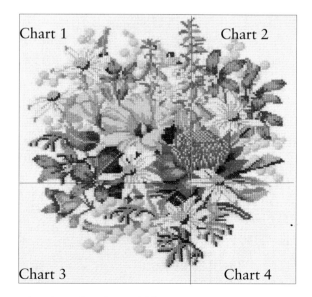

The chart for the Wildflower Bouquet has been split up into four sections as shown above.

Wildflower Bouquet 2

Wildflower Bouquet 2 - Chart 1

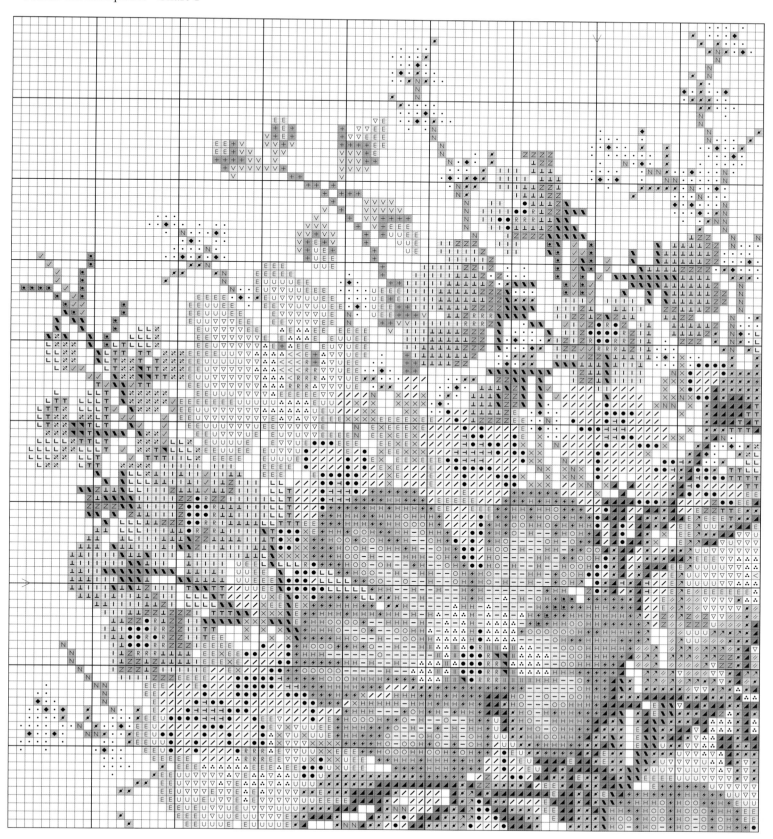

Wildflower Bouquet 2 - Chart 2

Key for DMC stranded cotton & tapestry wool:

Key for DMC stranded cotton & tapestry wool:

	cotton	wool			cotton	wool
· ·	white	ecru	⊣ ⊣		741	7437
⋇ ⋇	209	7895	∴ ∴		746	ecru
⋇ ⋇	210	7896	I I		758	7760
◢ ◢	320	7542	U U		776	7202
◢ ◢	333	7243	R R		783	7782
O O	340	7241	▽ ▽		818	7200
– –	341	7244	N N		840	7465
↗ ↗	347	7544	◤ ◤		895	7541
Z Z	355	7208	X X		906	7342
⊥ ⊥	356	7758	◖●		987	7320
◥ ◥	433	7496	✓ ✓		988	7384
● ●	444	7973	II II		3041	7266
╱ ╱	445	7434	+ +		3346	7386
V V	471	7376	◆ ◆		3687	7205
◣ ◣	550	7245	E E		3688	7204
T T	553	7708	⫽ ⫽		3712	7106
< <	726	7726	H H		3746	7711

Australian Hollyhock

Wildflower Bouquet 2 - Chart 3

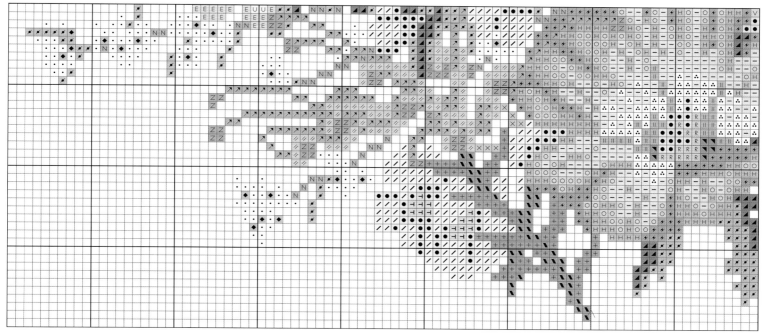

Stitch Count: 137 across
139 down

Wildflower Bouquet 2 - Chart 4

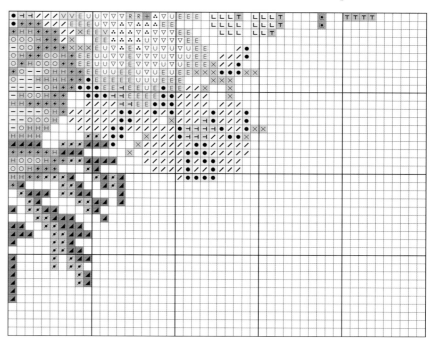

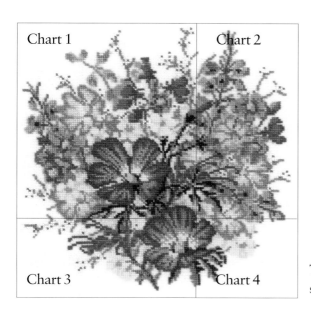

Chart 1   Chart 2

Chart 3   Chart 4

The chart for the **Wildflower Bouquet 2** has been
split up into four sections as shown on left.

Red-flowered Gum

Red-flowered Gum *(Eucalyptus ficifolia)*

A beautiful tree grown widely for its decorative purposes. The most common colour of the blossom is a rich scarlet-vermilion, but other colours range from pale pink to deep crimson.

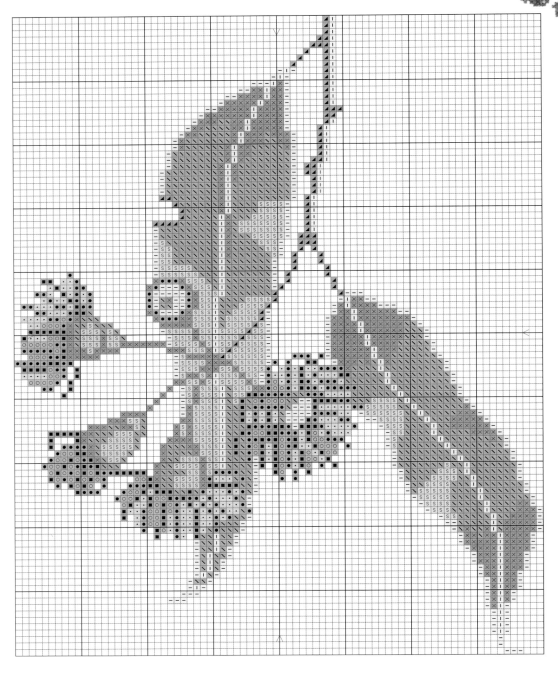

Key for DMC stranded cotton:

●	●	309
◢	◢	434
✕	✕	469
◥	◥	470
s	s	471
–	–	472
I	I	676
■	■	3685
○	○	3687
·	·	3688

Stitch Count: 80 across

100 down

Salmon Correa

Salmon Correa *(Correa pulchella)*

My favourite of all the correas. Growing in its natural habitat this lovely plant favours southern coastal areas. I have found this colourful little shrub growing on sheltered sandhills and also clinging precariously to windswept coastal cliff-faces.

Key for DMC stranded cotton:

● ●	● ●	347
· ·	· ·	760
✕ ✕	✕ ✕	839
✕ ✕	✕ ✕	840
■ ■	■ ■	840
◢ ◢	◢ ◢	895
↘ ↘	↘ ↘	3041
✕ ✕	✕ ✕	3042
○ ○	○ ○	3328
S S	S S	3345
B B	B B	3346
△ △	△ △	3347
– –	– –	3348
╱ ╱	╱ ╱	3712

Stamens have been highlighted by working small bullion stitches using one strand of DMC 743.

Stitch Count: 70 across
90 down

Native correas or native fuchsias are found only in Australia. They flower mainly in autumn and winter and are widely cultivated for gardens and parks.

Common Correa *(Correa reflexa)*, illustrated on right, grows in sandy soils.

Salmon Correa *(Correa pulchella)*, below, is embroidered on the previous page.

White Correa *(Correa alba)*, below right, grows along the south coast on limestone cliffs and is quite rare.

Spreading Correa

Spreading Correa (*Correa decumbens*), is a small shrub with tubular flowers that face upwards, unlike the other species of correas. Leaves are dark green with reddish hairs underneath. The brightly coloured flowers have eight protruding stamens. This plant is very rare.

Stitches and DMC Threads are given below for working this pretty Correa in Surface Stitchery:

Stems:	Work in **Stem stitch** with DMC 3012 and 3011.
Leaves:	Embroider the leaves with fine rows of **Chain stitch** using DMC 320, 367 and 319.
Petals:	Using DMC 3347, begin from the tips of the petals and gradually work down the flower tube in **Chain stitch**, changing colours to 3348, 3354, 3733, 3731, 3350, ending with the darkest red, 3685, at the base of the tube. **Stem stitch** the edges of the petals with DMC 3347.
Sepals:	The sepal cups of this correa are edged with a few irregular teeth. Work in **Chain stitch** with DMC 3348 and 3347, referring to the finished embroidery for shading and the teeth.
Filaments:	Work the long filaments in **Split stitch** using 3348.
Anthers:	Work the anthers in DMC 3829 using **Detached chain stitches.**

Birds of the Bush

Birds of the Bush

    Galah
    Superb Blue Wren
    New Holland Honeyeater
    Sacred Kingfisher
    Red-capped Robin
    Golden Whistler

Superb Blue Wren

Superb Blue Wren *(Malurus cyaneus)*

These little birds are mainly insect eaters and spend most of their time hopping and fossicking amongst the leaf litter on the ground in eucalypt woodland and open forests. In spring the dominant male changes his brown plumage to brilliant blue and black. They are very territorial and groups consist of several males, not all of them brilliantly coloured, with only the one female. The female mates with the dominant male only, and together they tolerate other males of their own kin and progeny. Females raised during breeding are driven from the group. All members of the group help to raise and feed the nestlings.

The Superb Blue Wren is shown here on a branch of **Flannel Flower.**

Key for DMC stranded cotton:

⋅ ⋅	white	U U	640	■ ■	895
I I	ecru	□ □	734	W W	927
I I	320	✕ ✕	782	▽ ▽	928
N N	333	▼ ▼	791	✕ ✕	930
← ←	368	+ +	813	▲ ▲	935
⚡ ⚡	413	↑ ↑	826	● ●	939
↖ ↖	414	\ \	827	◆ ◆	3012
○ ○	420	◄ ◄	838	✕ ✕	3013
– –	612	S S	842	⁒ ⁒	3021

Stitch Count: 120 across
160 down

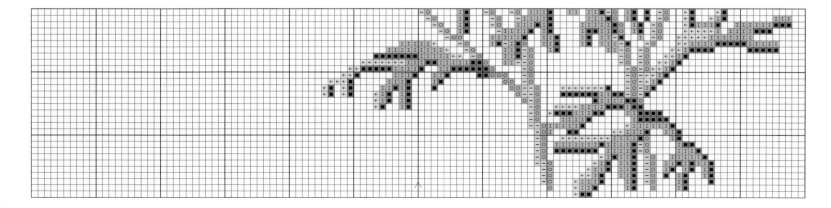

New Holland Honeyeater

New Holland Honeyeater *(Phylidonyris novaehollandiae)*
These colourful little birds are found in open forest and heathland. They visit gardens where flowering, nectar-rich native plants are grown, particularly banksias, grevilleas, dryandras and kangaroo paw flowers. They are noisy little birds and are easily identified by the yellow markings and white eyes.

Golden Wreath Wattle *(Acacia longifolia)*, is a very showy small tree with dark green pendulous foliage and an abundance of large, deep-golden heads.

Key for DMC stranded cotton:

white	743	937	840/726 (1 strand each)
310	780	3012	840/3022 (1 strand each)
413	782	3021	3021/839 (1 strand each)
415	783	3022	3021/3371 (1 strand each)
444	839	3024	
445	840	3346	
471	841	3371	
726	907	3721	
734	935	3827	

Stitch Count: 113 across
156 down

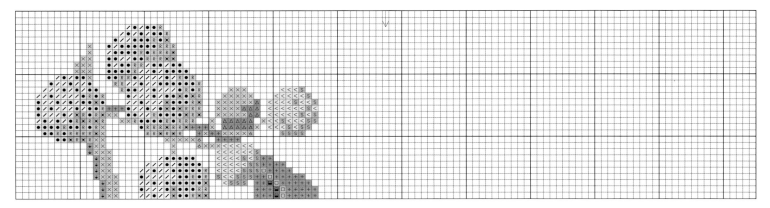

Red-capped Robin

Red-capped Robin *(Petroica goodenovii)*

These colourful little birds are continually restless, fluttering and twittering on low branches and on the ground among fallen twigs and leaves. Their diet of insects includes grasshoppers, beetles, flies, moths, bees and ants.

The Robin is shown here on a branch of Weeping Emubush *(Eremophila longifolia)*, a small shrub or tree widespread on the plains and ranges of the interior.

Key for DMC stranded cotton:

·· ··	white	>> >>	841
310		WW WW	927
** **	349	−− −−	928
433		II II	935
// //	445	→→ →→	939
722		++ ++	3328
33 33	760	3345
801		3346
838		3347
×× ××	839	// //	3348
○○ ○○	840	3371

Backstitching:

Backstitch around the four black eye stitches with 2 strands of DMC white.
Embroider stamens on the Weeping Emubush with one strand of DMC 3328.

Stitch Count: 66 across
  90 down

Sacred Kingfisher

Sacred Kingfisher *(Halcyon sancta)*

The beautiful little Sacred Kingfisher, sometimes called Green Kingfisher, is usually found near water, feeding on aquatic insects, small fish and reptiles.

Key for DMC stranded cotton:

white	▲▲	826
310	↑↑	839
318	∨∨	841
356	LL	930
414	HH	3051
436	CC	3053
501	××	3787
502	◤◥	3799
503	∇∇	826/841 (1 strand each)
734	◆◆	930/3799 (1 strand each)
738		

Stitch Count: 55 across

80 down

Backstitching: **eye**—work small backstitches around eye with two strands of DMC white

—highlight eye by working a tiny french knot with one strand of white

Branches—use two strands of DMC 839

Charley the Galah

Galah *(Eolophus roseicapilla)*

When we lived in the lower Barossa Valley we would often see 'Charley' flying around our home with his mate. Occasionally he would fly down and sit on our shoulders or at our feet with the greeting, 'Hello Charley!' At an earlier age he must have been caged and taught to talk.

Galahs are one of the most familiar of Australian parrots. Their favourite nesting sites are hollows in large eucalypt trees. Although farmers sometimes become upset at the damage they cause by eating the seed of their crops, galahs also devour large quantities of seeds of noxious plants.

This embroidery was designed from a photograph of Charley sitting on our daughter's shoulder. The blossom in the background is from the huge River Red Gums which grow in this area.

Stitch Count: 129 across
110 down

Key for DMC stranded cotton:

· ·	white	I I	676	⌐ ⌐	3041
▲ ▲	315	⌀ ⌀	734	↑ ↑	3042
6 6	316	⋏ ⋏	762	□ □	3346
C C	318	◣ ◣	801	\ \	3347
⤫ ⤫	355	U U	838	■ ■	3371
V V	356	O O	840	Z Z	3687
⁄ ⁄	371	> >	841	⁒ ⁒	3689
▽ ▽	414	◢ ◢	937	‖ ‖	3733
T T	610	L L	3011	− −	3823
H H	640	◆ ◆	3021		

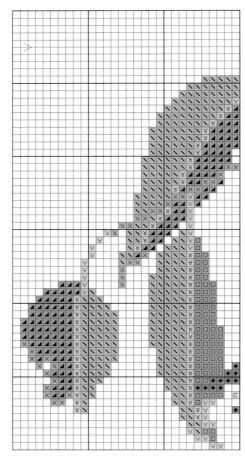

Backstitching:

Highlight the eye of the bird by working small backstitches around the eye as shown in the embroidery, using one strand of DMC 928.

Golden Whistler

Golden Whistler *(Pachycephala pectoralis)*
This little bird inhabits rainforest, scrub and open forest. Birds are found in pairs in the breeding season and singly or in loose wandering groups in the winter. Also called Yellow-breasted Whistler or Whipbird.

Change the colour of the blossom to suit your own taste. Creamy-white blossoms may show up the little bird better on a deeper coloured background fabric than the red embroidered here. You may prefer to delete the blossom under his beak

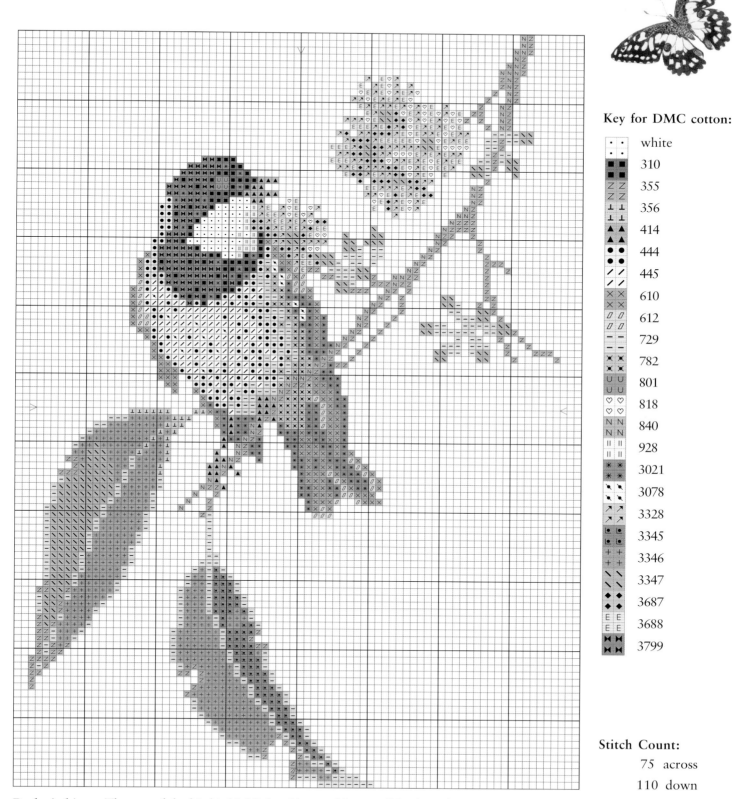

Key for DMC cotton:

· · / · ·		white
· / · · / ·		
■ ■ / ■ ■		310
Z Z / Z Z		355
⊥ ⊥ / ⊥ ⊥		356
▲ ▲ / ▲ ▲		414
● ● / ● ●		444
/ / / / /		445
✕ ✕ / ✕ ✕		610
∅ ∅ / ∅ ∅		612
– – / – –		729
✳ ✳ / ✳ ✳		782
U U / U U		801
♡ ♡ / ♡ ♡		818
N N / N N		840
‖ ‖ / ‖ ‖		928
✹ ✹ / ✹ ✹		3021
◤ ◥ / ◤ ◥		3078
↗ ↗ / ↗ ↗		3328
◖● / ◖●		3345
+ + / + +		3346
＼ ＼ / ＼ ＼		3347
◆ ◆ / ◆ ◆		3687
◆ ◆ / ◆ ◆		3688
E E / E E		3688
◤◥ / ◤◥		3799

Stitch Count:

75 across

110 down

Backstitching: The eye of the bird is highlighted by working small backstitches around the eye as shown in the embroidery, using one strand of DMC 928.

Ground Orchids

Native ground orchids have a very special magic for me. These beautiful, fragile little plants have to struggle to survive in the few remaining pieces of natural forest and bushland. Many orchids are now extinct or close to extinction.

They have been given such wonderful names, for example, fairy orchid, spider orchid, blue or pink fairies, mosquito orchid, donkey orchid, rabbit-ears, and the list goes on. It is quite evident that they also had a special magic for whoever gave them their common names.

The painting on the left page shows the dainty **Mayfly Orchid** *(Acianthus caudatus)* and a spider orchid, **Daddy-long-legs** *(Caladenia filamentosa)*. The small Ivy-leafed Violet *(Viola hederaceae)*, is shown nestled amongst the leaf litter between them. In the background is the woody fruit of the Silver Banksia *(Banksia marginata)*, covered in yellow fungi.

Illustrations on this page are studies of the Nodding Greenhood *(Pterostylis nutans)*.

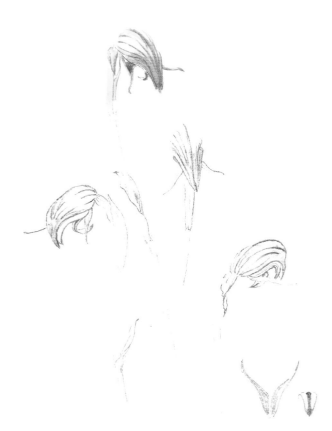

Blue Fairies

Blue Fairies *(Caladenia deformis)*
These beautiful little orchids are seen in late winter and early spring. They are found in a wide range of areas from the coast to the forest, often growing together in small clumps. The single flowers range in colour from a brilliant blue through to occasionally white.

The painting opposite shows the Blue Fairies growing around a clump of small lilies, Blue Stars *(Chamaescilla corymbosa)*. In the background is a tiny Cinnamon Donkey Orchid, *(Diuris palustris)*.

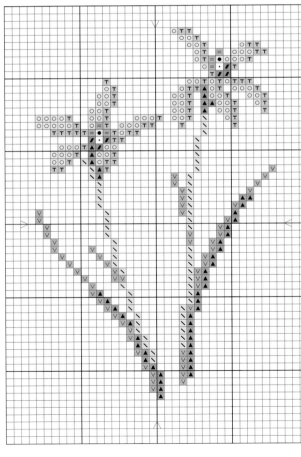

Key for DMC stranded cotton:

· ·	· ·	white
O O	O O	341
⁄ ⁄	⁄ ⁄	550
● ●	● ●	725
T T	T T	793
▲ ▲	▲ ▲	3346
V V	V V	3347
\ \	\ \	3348
= =	= =	3837

Stitch Count: 32 across
48 down

Helmet Orchids

Veined Helmet Orchid *(Corybas dilatatus)*

Helmet Orchids are dwarf plants with flat green leaves, and are usually found in quite large colonies in damp, sheltered areas. Only a small proportion of these plants will flower during winter.

The painting below shows a group of Veined Helmet Orchids sheltering in deep shade at the base of a Xanthorrhoea or grass tree. To photograph them I had to use a flashlight on my camera and lie on my stomach on the damp forest floor.

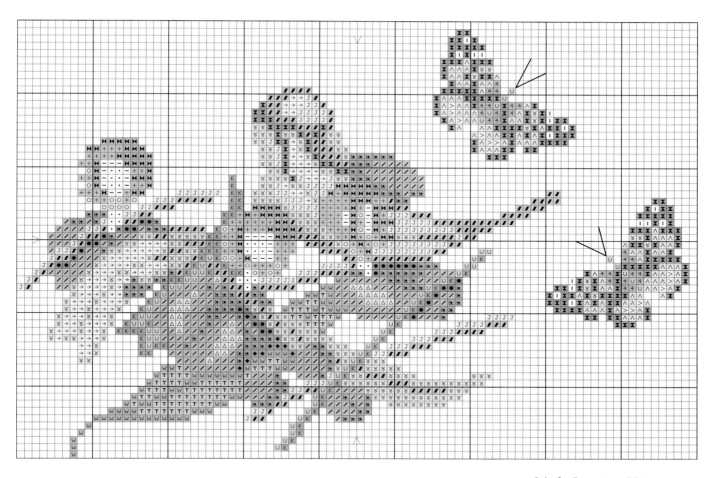

Stitch Count: 89 across
59 down

Key for DMC stranded cotton:

I I / I I	ecru
− − / − −	225
◆ ◆ / ◆ ◆	300
O O / O O	316
> > / > >	341
W W / W W	355
T T / T T	356
∕∕ / ∕∕	420
J J / J J	422
4 4 / 4 4	434
→ → / → →	676
⋈ ⋈ / ⋈ ⋈	729

· · / · ·	746
✗ ✗ / ✗ ✗	801
K K / K K	839
U U / U U	841
∧ ∧ / ∧ ∧	977
● ● / ● ●	3345
⦿ ⦿ / ⦿ ⦿	3346
∕ ∕ / ∕ ∕	3347
△ △ / △ △	3348
+ + / + +	3726
■ ■ / ■ ■	3781
⋈ ⋈ / ⋈ ⋈	3802

Butterfly feelers are embroidered in
backstitch with one strand of DMC 801

Fire Orchids

Fire Orchids *(Pyrorchis nigricans)*

Great communities of the leaves of these orchids are often found in habitats ranging from coastal sandhills to dense forests. Flowering is usually infrequent except after bushfires (hence the name 'Fire Orchid'), when quite spectacular displays are produced.

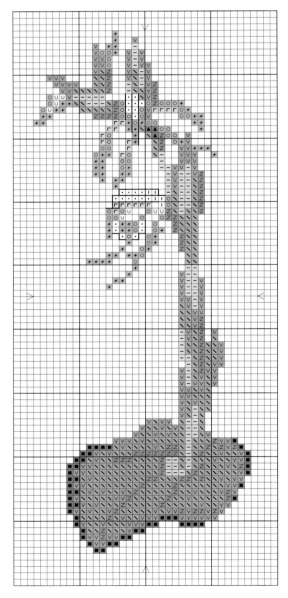

Key for DMC stranded cotton:

·· ··	white
V V V V	315
I I I I	746
■ ■ ■ ■	902
▲ ▲ ▲ ▲	3345
Z Z Z Z	3346
\ \ \ \	3347
– – – –	3348
O O O O	3687
Γ Γ Γ Γ	3688
U U U U	3689
✦ ✦ ✦ ✦	3803

Backstitch around white stitches with one strand of DMC 3687

Stitch Count: 33 across
  82 down

58

Spring Orchids

The colourful orchids embroidered here were found growing in close proximity to each other in an open area of eucalypt forest that had been cleared of larger trees and shrubs a few years earlier.

Narrow-Lipped Spider Orchid *(Caladenia leptochila)*
Hare Orchids *(Leptoceras menziesii)*
Cockatoos *(Glossodia major)*
Yellow Stars *(Hypoxis glabella)*, do not belong to the Orchid family.

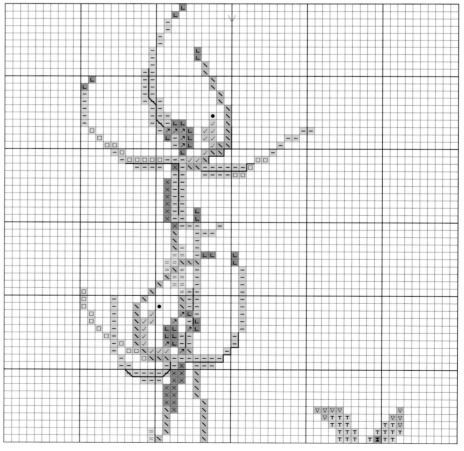

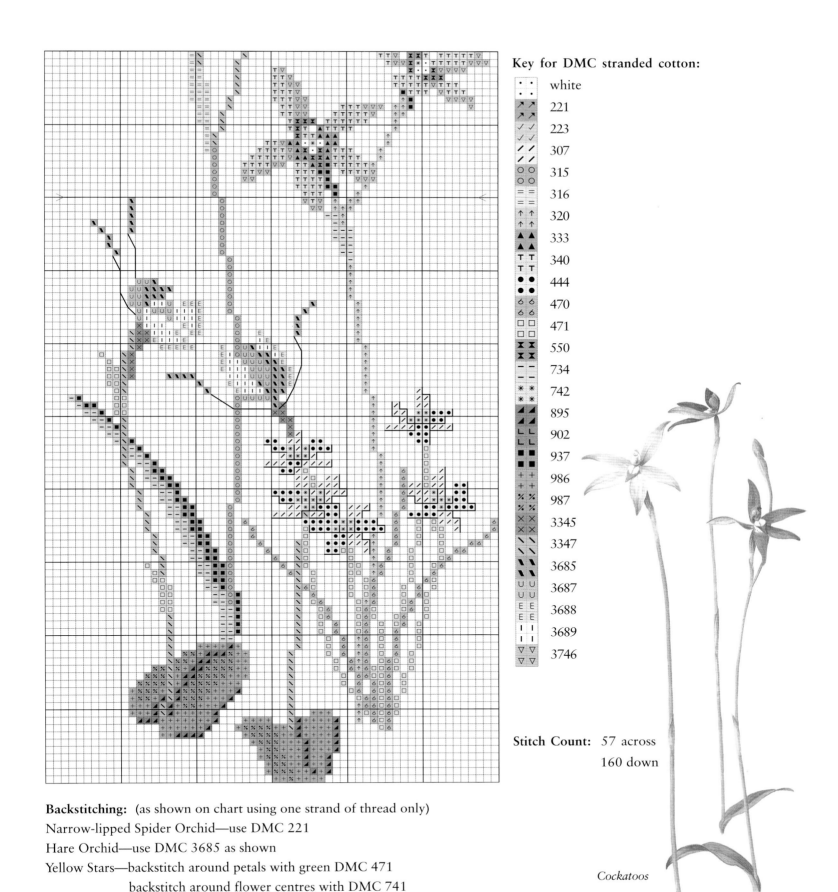

Key for DMC stranded cotton:

· ·	white
↗ ↗	221
✓ ✓	223
╱ ╱	307
○ ○	315
= =	316
↑ ↑	320
▲ ▲	333
T T	340
● ●	444
6 6	470
□ □	471
✗ ✗	550
▬ ▬	734
− −	742
✳ ✳	742
◢ ◢	895
L L	902
■ ■	937
+ +	986
‰ ‰	987
⤫ ⤫	3345
⤬ ⤬	3347
◣ ◣	3685
U U	3687
E E	3688
I I	3689
▽ ▽	3746

Stitch Count: 57 across
160 down

Cockatoos

Backstitching: (as shown on chart using one strand of thread only)
Narrow-lipped Spider Orchid—use DMC 221
Hare Orchid—use DMC 3685 as shown
Yellow Stars—backstitch around petals with green DMC 471
backstitch around flower centres with DMC 741

The **Narrow-Lipped Spider Orchid** (*Caladenia leptochila*), is sometimes called 'Queen Spider', no doubt because of its erect and upward curving sepals.

Hare Orchids (*Leptoceras menziesii*), have attractive pink and white fragrant flowers and large green leaves.

The **Greenhood** (*Pterostylis pedunculata*), is commonly found in forest and coastal heath.

Cockatoos (*Glossodia major*) range in colour from mauve or purple to occasionally white, and can form spectacular displays in the forest (illustrated on previous page).

The little **Yellow Stars** (*Hypoxis glabella*) and **Blue Stars** (*Chamaescilla corymbosa*) painted here do not belong to the Orchid family.

The Cockatoos bring back vivid memories. I stopped one hot day on a narrow track in the forest to admire a large group of these colourful orchids. The sunlight was filtering down through the trees highlighting the varying colours of their 'petals'. I became aware of a slight movement further down the track, and looked up to see a huge brown snake, head raised, waiting to strike. If I had not stopped to admire this display I would have walked right into the snake. Trying not to panic I slowly backed away. I can't say I enjoyed the remainder of my walk that day, but it did teach me to be more careful of where I was treading.

Opposite page: A group of **Mosquito Orchids** (*Acianthus pusillus*). During late winter, in damp sheltered areas of the forest, great colonies of small, flat, heart-shaped green leaves appear, nestling in between leaf litter and moss. Only a small percentage of these plants actually flower.

Greenhood Orchids

Dwarf Greenhoods *(Pterostylis nana)*

These tiny little orchids flower in late winter in sheltered positions under trees and bushes. Their non-fragrant flowers are pale green, and the leaves grow in basal rosettes.

The painting on the opposite page shows the Dwarf Greenhoods with associated plants. From left to right: Early Nancy *(Wurmbea dioica)*, Yellow Stars *(Hypoxis glabella)*, Rock Fern *(Cheilanthes austrotenuifolia)*, Scented Sundew *(Drosera whittakeri)* and Blue Stars *(Chamaescilla corymbosa)*.

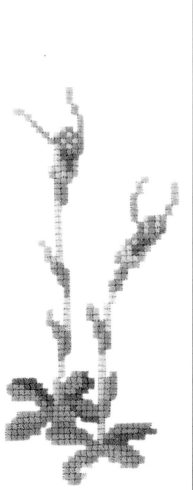

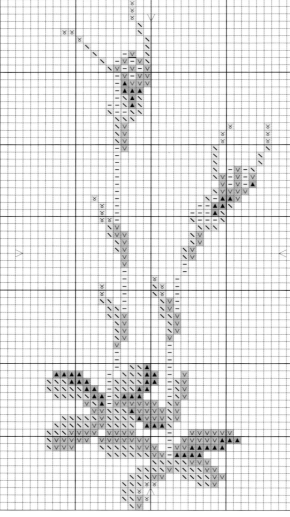

Key for DMC stranded cotton:

V V	470
\ \	471
– –	472
⌧ ⌧	729
▲ ▲	937

Stitch Count: 30 across
70 down

Jan Woodman
2001

65

Collection of Orchids

This collection of orchids features three of the 'Sun orchids', so-called because of the need for full sun for their flowers to open.

The largest here is the **Tall Sun-Orchid** *(Thelymitra grandiflora)* which has many blue or mauve flowers on a tall spike.

Scented Sun-Orchid *(Thelymitra nuda)* has fewer flowers on a spike and is found in a much larger range of habitat. The blue, mauve or sometimes white flowers are sweetly scented.

Rabbit Ears *(Thelymitra antennifera)* is a small orchid with one to four bright yellow flowers on a slender stem.

The other orchids embroidered here are:

King Spider Orchid *(Caladenia tentaculata)*

Cockatoos *(Glossodia major)*

Hare Orchid *(Leptoceras menziesii)*

Backstitching:
King Spider Orchid—one strand of DMC 3721
Hare Orchid—one strand of DMC 3687
Rabbit Orchid—one strand of DMC 3347

Key for DMC stranded cotton:

Symbol	Color		Symbol	Color
· ·	white		ʎ ʎ	3042
◐ ◐	208		▼ ▼	3346
⊠ ⊠	209		\ \	3347
L L	210		✓ ✓	3348
/ /	221		▲ ▲	3685
C C	223		Z Z	3687
⊠ ⊠	224		■ ■	3721
O O	307		↘ ↘	3743
◤ ◤	327		✕ ✕	3746
◨ ◨	333		✳ ✳	3803
▽ ▽	340		˥ ˥	3819
˥ ˥	341		+ +	3827
● ●	444			
V V	471			
− −	472			
A A	503			
◣ ◣	550			
★ ★	552			
N N	553			
⁰ ⁰	554			
2 2	727			
✗ ✗	729			
< <	743			
U U	792			
↓ ↓	793			
M M	794			
◆ ◆	814			
W W	927			
↑ ↑	976			
F F	987			
H H	989			

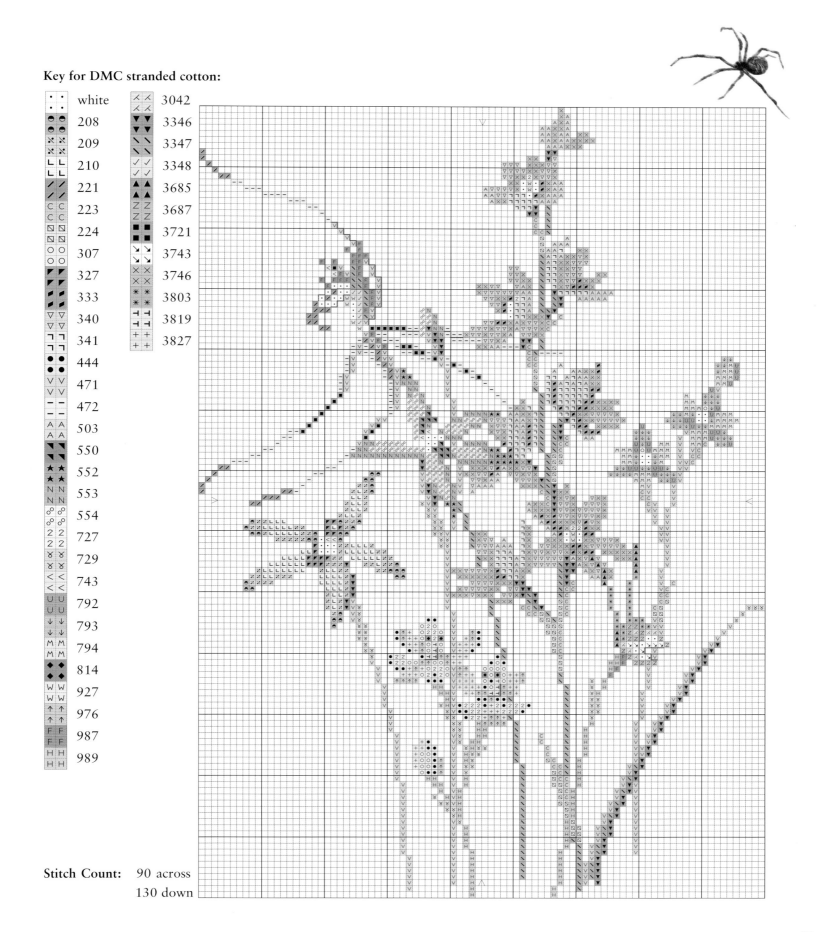

Stitch Count: 90 across

130 down

Chocolate Lily
(*Arthropodium strictus*)

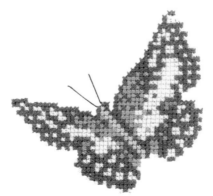

Butterflies

Checkered Swallowtail
Common Eggfly
Common Imperial Blue
Green-banded Blues
Lesser Wanderer
Macleay's Swallowtail
Male Wood White
Monarch
Tailed Emperor

Butterfly Bellpull

Butterflies:

Green-banded Blues
Checkered Swallowtail
Macleay's Swallowtail
Male Wood White
Lesser Wanderer
Common Imperial Blue
Monarch
Tailed Emperor
Common Eggfly

Wildflowers:

Nodding Blue Lily *(Stypandra glauca)*
Boronia *(Boronia inornata)*
Pink-eyed Susan *(Tetratheca pilosa)*
Common Buttercup *(Ranunculus lappaceus)*
Downy Mintbush *(Prostanthera behriana)*
Blue Pincushion *(Brunonia australis)*
Tea-tree *(Leptospermum sp.)*

Butterfly Bellpull Chart 1

Butterfly Bellpull Chart 3

Butterfly Bellpull Chart 4

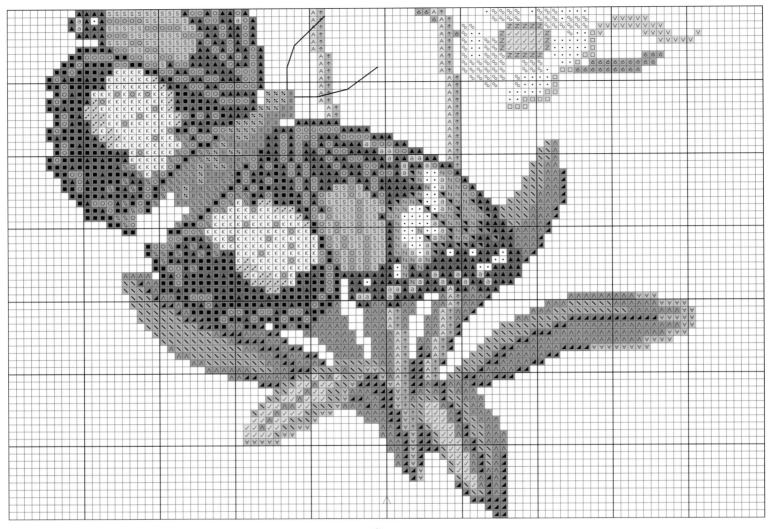

Stitch Count: 96 across
400 down

Butterfly feelers:
Embroider all butterfly feelers in backstitch using
one strand of DMC 3371.

Painting on left: Blue Boronia (*Boronia coerulescens*)
Painting opposite: Checkered Swallowtail and Bulbine Lily (*Bulbine bulbosa*)

Key for DMC stranded cotton:

⋮⋮	white	>>	841
U U	ecru	I I	919
✳ ✳	208	W W	927
✕ ✕	209	a a	932
⫶ ⫶	211	= =	975
C C	223	→ →	976
◨ ◨	224	↓ ↓	977
△ △	225	✗ ✗	987
◇ ◇	307	F F	988
⊕ ⊕	312	H H	989
◆ ◆	327	L L	3021
➢ ➢	334	∩ ∩	3022
⌐ ⌐	341	⁒ ⁒	3032
S S	351	◣ ◣	3078
⩡ ⩡	356	⋰ ⋰	3325
← ←	368	◢ ◢	3345
◫ ◫	434	∧ ∧	3346
● ●	444	＼ ＼	3347
╱ ╱	445	✓ ✓	3348
6 6	470	▲ ▲	3371
V V	471	Z Z	3687
↑ ↑	502	□ □	3688
A A	503	⁰⁄₀ ⁰⁄₀	3689
◤ ◤	550	E E	3722
N N	553	Ǝ Ǝ	3768
K K	677	‖ ‖	3781
⋰ ⋰	722	➤ ➤	3816
◥ ◥	801	4 4	3820
▽ ▽	813	− −	3822
T T	823	▼ ▼	3826
▼ ▼	825	◀ ◀	3834
✕ ✕	827	⬝⬝ ⬝⬝	3835
■ ■	838	◿ ◿	3836
○ ○	840		

CHECKERED SWALLOWTAIL Butterflies

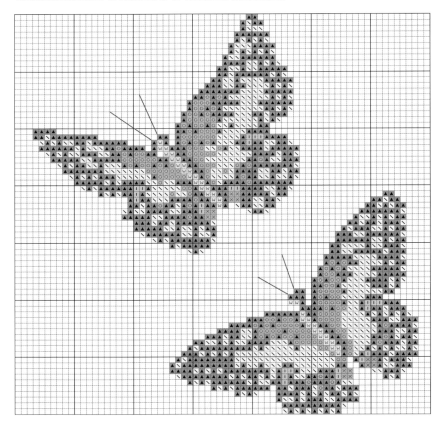

Key for DMC stranded cotton:

✕ ✕		355
I I		826
○ ○		840
W W		927
▲ ▲		3021
⟍ ⟍		3078

Feelers are embroidered with one strand of DMC 3021

MONARCH Butterfly

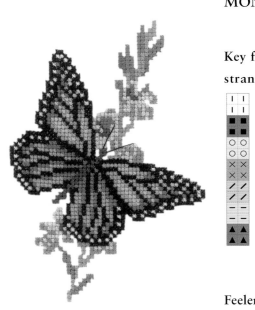
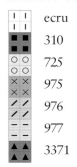

Key for DMC stranded cotton:

I I		ecru
■ ■		310
○ ○		725
✕ ✕		975
╱ ╱		976
— —		977
▲ ▲		3371

Feelers are embroidered with one strand of DMC 3371

Male and Female WOOD WHITE Butterflies

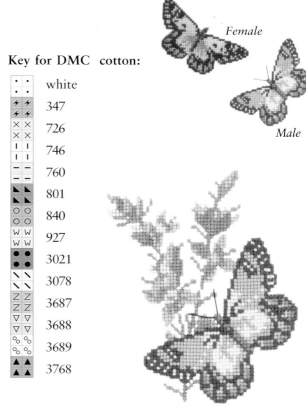

Female

Male

Key for DMC cotton:

· · / · ·	white	
ϟ ϟ / ϟ ϟ	347	
✕ ✕ / ✕ ✕	726	
∣ ∣ / ∣ ∣	746	
− − / − −	760	
◣ ◣ / ◣ ◣	801	
○ ○ / ○ ○	840	
W W / W W	927	
● ● / ● ●	3021	
＼ ＼ / ＼ ＼	3078	
Z Z / Z Z	3687	
▽ ▽ / ▽ ▽	3688	
° ° / ° °	3689	
▲ ▲ / ▲ ▲	3768	

Feelers are embroidered with one strand of DMC 3021

LESSER WANDERER Butterfly

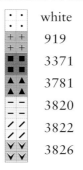

Key for DMC stranded cotton:

· · / · ·	white	
+ + / + +	919	
■ ■ / ■ ■	3371	
▲ ▲ / ▲ ▲	3781	
− − / − −	3820	
∕ ∕ / ∕ ∕	3822	
⌄ ⌄ / ⌄ ⌄	3826	

Feelers are embroidered with one strand of DMC 3781

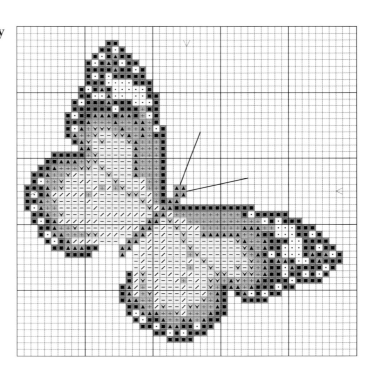

LARGE GREEN-BANDED BLUE Butterflies

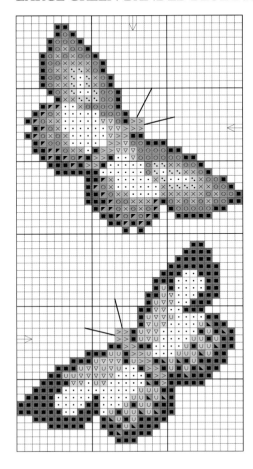

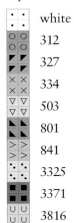

Key for DMC stranded cotton:

· · / · ·	white
O O / O O	312
◣ ◢ / ◣ ◢	327
X X / X X	334
▽ ▽ / ▽ ▽	503
◣ ◤ / ◢ ◥	801
> > / > >	841
· · / · ·	3325
■ ■ / ■ ■	3371
U U / U U	3816

Feelers are embroidered with one strand of DMC 3371

TAILED EMPEROR Butterfly

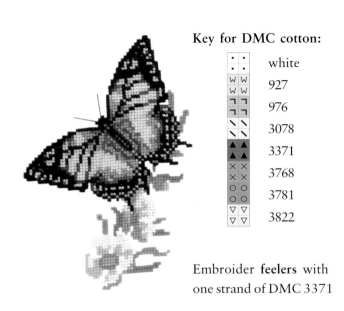

Key for DMC cotton:

· · / · ·	white
W W / W W	927
˥ ˥ / ˥ ˥	976
\ \ / \ \	3078
▲ ▲ / ▲ ▲	3371
X X / X X	3768
O O / O O	3781
▽ ▽ / ▽ ▽	3822

Embroider **feelers** with
one strand of DMC 3371

COMMON IMPERIAL BLUE Butterfly

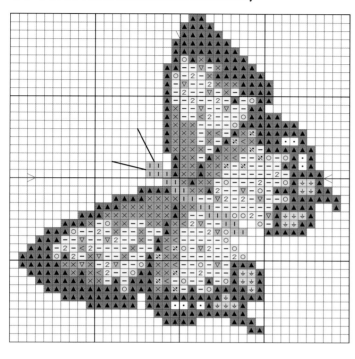

Key for DMC stranded cotton:

Symbol	DMC
· · / · ·	white
✕ ✕ / ✕ ✕	209
2 2 / 2 2	727
O O / O O	813
▲ ▲ / ▲ ▲	823
✕ ✕ / ✕ ✕	825
− − / − −	827
↓ ↓ / ↓ ↓	977
▽ ▽ / ▽ ▽	988
I I / I I	3022
< < / < <	3760

Feelers are embroidered with one strand of DMC 3022

MACLEAY'S SWALLOWTAIL Butterfly

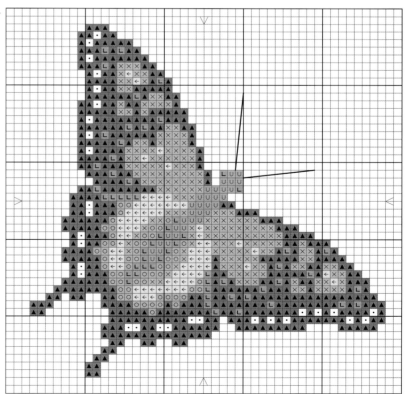

Key for DMC stranded cotton:

Symbol	DMC
· · / · ·	white
← ← / ← ←	368
O O / O O	840
✕ ✕ / ✕ ✕	988
▲ ▲ / ▲ ▲	3371
U U / U U	3768
L L / L L	3781

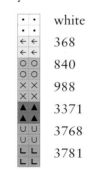

Feelers are embroidered with one strand of DMC 3781

COMMON EGGFLY Butterfly

Key for DMC stranded cotton:

· ·	white	× ×	838
S S	351	O O	840
◨	434	− −	932
◣	550	╲╲	3032
N N	553	■ ■	3371
K K	677	U U	3781
╱ ╱	722		

Butterfly feelers are embroidered in
backstitch using one strand of DMC 3371.

Blue-banded Eggfly Butterfly

The Blue-banded Eggfly Butterfly is embroidered here on a branch
of **Blue Fanflower** *(Scaevola calendulaceae)*, a beautiful ground-
cover plant found mainly on the coast.

Key for DMC stranded cotton:

white			3021
327		◆	3345
341		×	3346
472		\	3347
517		■	3371
N 553		=	3740
554		U	3746
801		T	3755
> 841			

Stitch Count: 60 across
                   79 down

The brilliant lustrous effect of blue on the butterfly wings was achieved by using one strand of Kreinik Metallic
Balger blending filament, 014HL with two strands of the blue colours 3755 and 517.
Butterfly feelers are embroidered in backstitch using one strand of DMC 801.

Three-dimensional butterflies:

Three-dimensional butterflies can be used in many ways. A card for a special occasion looks even more special with a hand-worked butterfly attached. Embellish a box top or gift by placing an embroidered butterfly on top. Sometimes a framed piece of work is enhanced with a butterfly on the mount.

Embroider the butterfly on a tightly woven background fabric, remembering that the finer the fabric the smaller the butterfly will be. Aida 18 is ideal for this purpose. If you decide to use Aida 18 and are working a pale coloured butterfly you might only need to use one strand of thread, but if the butterfly is deeper in colour use two strands to achieve the deep velvet richness of the wings. Be very careful not to carry threads across the back of areas that will not be stitched.

When you have finished cross-stitching your butterfly, lightly glue the back of the embroidery with either a good aerosol art glue or a non-stainable craft glue. When dry attach a double sided iron-on adhesive to the back of the embroidery with your iron. Before peeling off the paper back of the adhesive, carefully cut out the butterfly, keeping as close to the stitching as you can without cutting the embroidery threads. Now peel off the paper backing.

Feelers can be made out of fine fuse wire which has been tightly wrapped with one strand of cotton, or out of tiny flower stamens which are available in different colours from most craft shops.

Use Blending Filaments to add sparkle:

A sparkling lustrous effect can be achieved on the butterfly wings by incorporating blending filaments with your embroidery threads. Do not overdo it by using the sparkly thread with every colour - just select three or four areas to highlight your design.

Blending filaments are not easy to work with as they do not move through the fabric as easily as stranded cotton. Use short lengths to prevent it from splitting and tangling, and always dampen the blending filament before using it.

Surface Stitchery

I have had many comments from embroiderers using my previous books saying that they delight in using my paintings as a basis for surface embroidery. On the following pages I have included ideas for converting flowers into simple surface stitchery.

All these designs were worked on a tightly woven background fabric using DMC stranded cottons.

Blue Pincushion

The flower heads of the dainty Blue Pincushion are made up of masses of tiny blue flowers, each little flower consisting of five petals with a protruding yellow style.

Daisy stitch was chosen here for the petals, using varying shades of blue, with French knots for the yellow styles. The velvety basal leaves were embroidered with closely worked rows of Chain stitch, and the stems and sepals worked in Stem stitch.

Scented Sundew

Scented Sundew *(Drosera whittakeri)*
Sundews are delightful little plants found late winter and early spring while the ground is still damp. They range from tiny plants with leaves in a basal rosette to long twining plants with leaves along the stem. Usually found in poor soil their food supply is supplemented with insects caught by the sticky gland-tipped hairs which cover the leaves.

The **Scented Sundew** is a tiny perennial herb with bronze, red or green leaves in a basal rosette. The large white, scented flowers grow singly on short stems.

Blanket stitch was chosen here for the petals with French knots for the stamens and Satin stitch for the flower centre. The leaves were embroidered with close rows of Chain stitch and then outlined in Stem stitch.

Native Primrose

Native Primrose *(Goodenia blackiana)*

This small perennial plant grows in quite large groups in forests and woodlands. The flowers grow singly on stems and have five deep yellow winged petals. The leaves grow mostly in a basal rosette.

Closed Fly stitch was used for the centre of the petals and Satin stitch for the wings. The leaves were embroidered in Slanted Satin stitch, with a row of Stem stitch to outline the central vein.

Scaly Buttons

Scaly Buttons *(Leptorhynchos squamatus)*

This little plant belongs to the daisy family and is found in many habitats from the forest to the coast.

Masses of French knots in varying thicknesses and shades of yellow were embroidered here to form the flower heads. Stem stitch was used for the stems and the narrow leaves were embroidered with close rows of Chain stitch.

Early Nancy

Early Nancy *(Wurmbia dioica)*

A member of the lily family, this little plant is widespread in many habitats, flowering in early spring. The white flowers have maroon markings and are sweetly-scented.

The flower petals were worked in Satin stitch and Daisy stitch, with French knots on stalks for the stamens. The long strap-like leaves were embroidered with close rows of Chain stitch.

More Wildflowers

Australian Floral Emblems:

- **Golden Wattle** *(Australia)*
- **Royal Bluebell** *(Australian Capital Territory)*
- **Waratah** *(New South Wales)*
- **Kangaroo Paw** *(Western Australia)*
- **Common Heath** *(Victoria)*
- **Cooktown Orchid** *(Queensland)*
- **Sturt's Desert Rose** *(Northern Territory)*
- **Sturt's Desert Pea** *(South Australia)*
- **Tasmanian Blue Gum** *(Tasmania)*

Golden Wattle

Golden Wattle *(Acacia pycnantha)*

The brilliant-yellow, fragrant flowers of Golden Wattle make it a very showy and well-known small tree. Flowering in spring large fluffy flowerheads make a vivid contrast against the dark foliage.

The early settlers interwove the long flexible twigs of Golden Wattle and daubed them with mud to make the framework of their houses. Trees are also grown commercially for the high content of tannin in their bark.

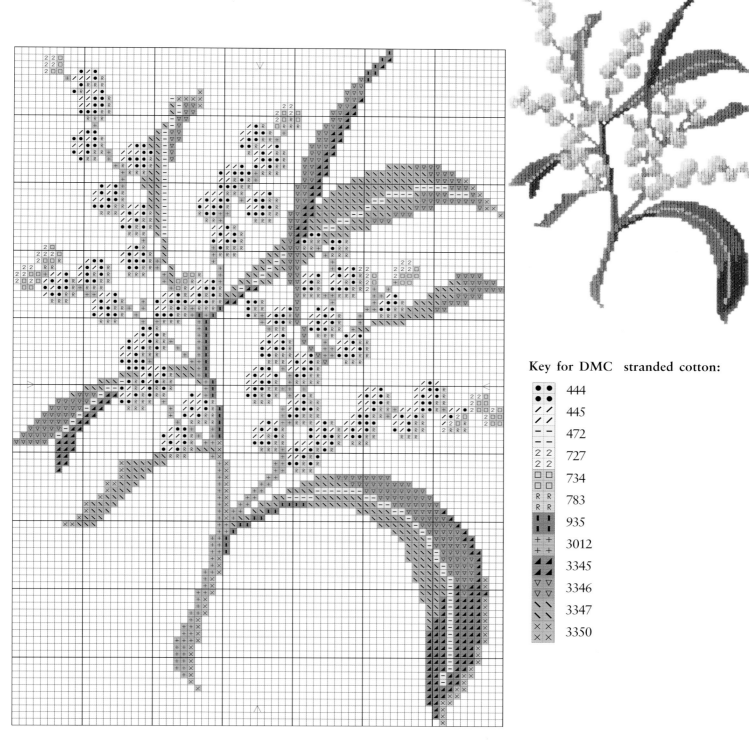

Stitch Count: 69 across
100 down

Key for DMC stranded cotton:

● ●	444
● ●	445
∕ ∕	472
– –	727
2 2	734
□ □	783
R R	935
∎ ∎	3012
+ +	3345
◢ ◢	3346
▽ ▽	3347
＼ ＼	3350
✕ ✕	

Royal Bluebell

Royal Bluebell *(Wahlenbergia gloriosa)*

A delightful small, perennial herb with rich violet-blue flowers carried erect or nodding on slender stems. The shining, oblong leaves have bluntly toothed and waved margins. They occur mainly in sub-alpine woodland.

Key for DMC stranded cotton:

· ·	white
\ \	209
I I	211
● ●	333
O O	340
⌐ ⌐	341
6 6	470
V V	471
− −	472
✕ ✕	782
▼ ▼	791
■ ■	935
✦ ✦	3045
Y Y	3046
✕ ✕	3350

Stitch Count: 60 across
130 down

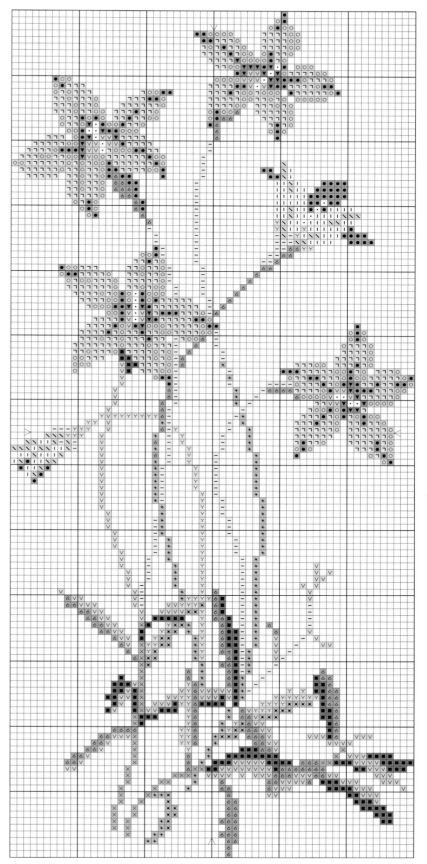

Waratah

Waratah *(Telopea speciosissima)*
A brilliantly coloured erect shrub. The dark green, leathery leaves are alternately arranged and coarsely toothed. The flowers are grouped in large, rounded heads, surrounded by crimson bracts.

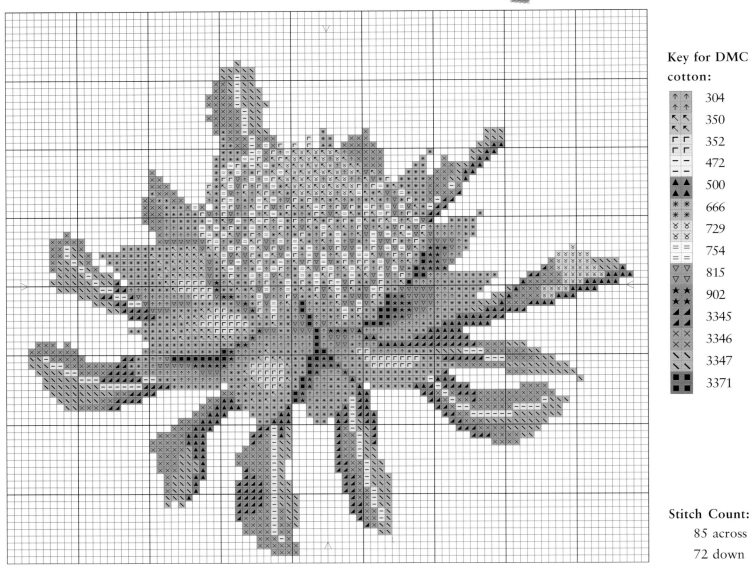

Key for DMC cotton:

Symbol	DMC
↑ ↑	304
↖ ↖	350
Γ Γ	352
– –	472
▲ ▲	500
✳ ✳	666
⊗ ⊗	729
= =	754
▽ ▽	815
★ ★	902
◢ ◣	3345
✕ ✕	3346
╲ ╲	3347
■ ■	3371

Stitch Count:
85 across
72 down

Kangaroo Paw

Kangaroo Paw *(Anigozanthos manglesii)*

A low shrub with broad leaves that taper to an acute point. The flowering stem and base of the flowers are deep red, covered with woolly hairs. The colour of the flower then changes to bright green, splitting to reveal yellow anthers.

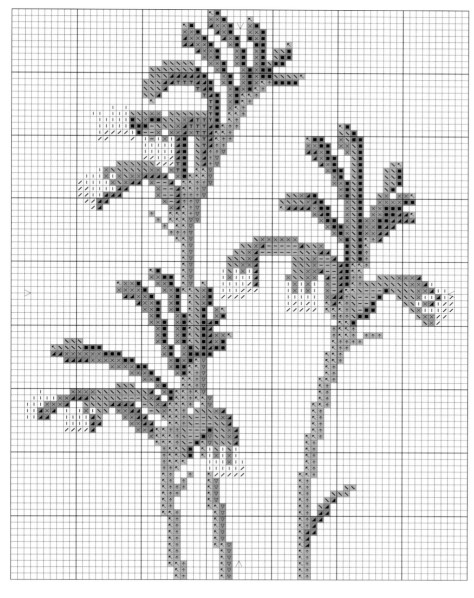

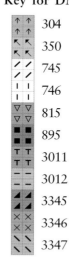

Key for DMC stranded cotton:

↑ ↑	304
↖ ↖	350
⁄ ⁄	745
⌐ ⌐	746
▽ ▽	815
■ ■	895
T T	3011
− −	3012
◣ ◣	3345
× ×	3346
＼ ＼	3347

Stitch Count: 66 across
90 down

Common Heath

Common Heath *(Epacris impressa)*
A colourful slender, upright shrub. Leaves are rigid, alternate and
sharply pointed. The tubular flowers range in colour from white or
pale pink, to deep crimson.

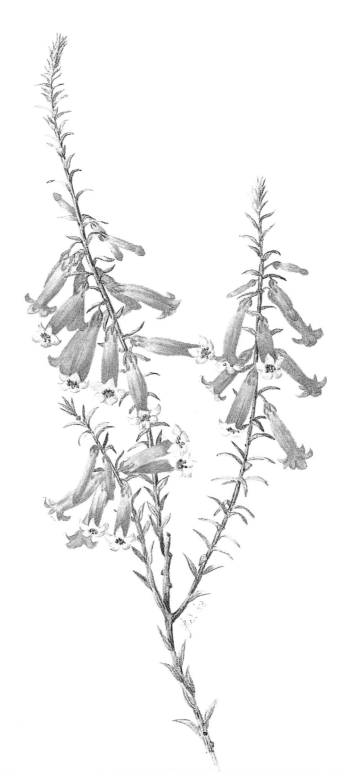

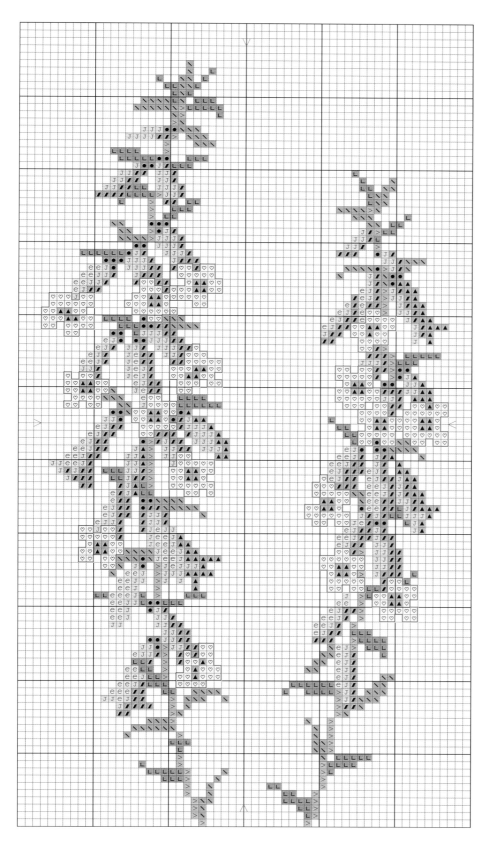

Key for DMC stranded cotton:

✐✐ / ✐✐	309
●● / ●●	355
♡♡ / ♡♡	818
>> / >>	841
JJ / JJ	899
ee / ee	3326
LL / LL	3346
\\ / \\	3347
▲▲ / ▲▲	3350

Backstitch around edges of pale pink petals with one strand of DMC 899.

Stitch Count: 54 across
105 down

Cooktown Orchid

Cooktown Orchid *(Dendrobium bigibbum)*

The Cooktown Orchid grows in exposed situations, either attached to tree trunks or on rocky outcrops, and is not a rainforest species. Flowering stems carry up to twenty stalked flowers which are usually deep lilac in colour.

Key for DMC

stranded cotton:

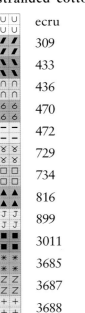

U	ecru
∕	309
∖	433
∩	436
6	470
–	472
⋈	729
□	734
▲	816
J	899
■	3011
✳	3685
Z	3687
+	3688
⁰	3689

Stitch Count: 53 across
120 down

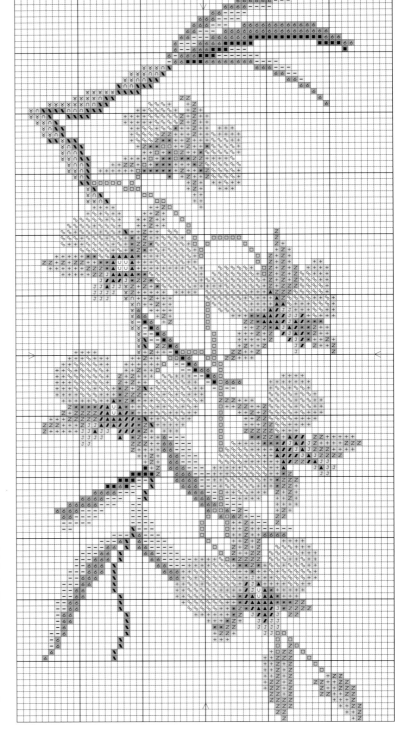

Sturt's Desert Rose

Sturt's Desert Rose *(Gossypium sturtianum)*
The natural habitat of Sturt's Desert Rose are stony slopes and dry creek beds. Flowers have pinky-mauve petals with red bases, forming a contrasting centre in each flower. This attractive bush occurs throughout most of Australia.

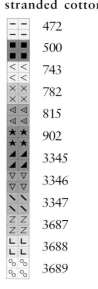

Key for DMC stranded cotton:

Symbol	DMC
– –	472
■ ■	500
< <	743
× ×	782
◁ ◁	815
★ ★	902
◢ ◢	3345
▽ ▽	3346
\ \	3347
Z Z	3687
L L	3688
∘ ∘	3689

Stitch Count: 69 across
60 down

Sturt's Desert Pea

Sturt's Desert Pea *(Swainsona formosa)*

A brilliantly coloured and very distinctive creeper. The stems and grey-green leaves are covered in downy hairs. Flowers are arranged in clusters of six to eight on short, thick, erect stalks. Petals are usually scarlet with a glossy black swelling at the base of the uppermost petal. Other colour forms range in colour from white to deep pink. After a good season on the dry outback plains, great carpets of these spectacular plants can be seen flowering for long periods during late winter and spring.

Key for DMC cotton:

U	ecru
↑	304
I	320
S	351
Γ	352
V	471
A	503
✳	666
△	815
◆	895
★	902
▲	937
⊥	3013
=	3052
■	3371
✕	3721

Tasmanian Blue Gum

Tasmanian Blue Gum *(Eucalyptus globulus)*

A tall, straight tree with rough, persistent bark at the base and smooth bark above. The cream flowers produce nectar in copious quantities yielding strongly flavoured honey. Mature leaves are dark, shining green. The name 'Blue Gum' is derived from the blue-grey, waxy bloom covering the juvenile leaves.

Key for DMC

stranded cotton:

$ $	355
∀ ∀	356
◐ ◑	420
/ /	445
∨ ∨	471
◢ ◪	500
◆ ◆	502
∧ ∧	504
▽ ▽	676
□ □	734
I I	746
= =	3052
✦ ✦	3078
⬡ ⬡	3362

Stitch Count: 58 across
128 down

Wreath of Wildflowers

Golden Wattle
Royal Bluebell
Waratah
Common Heath
Cooktown Orchid
Sturt's Desert Pea
Sturt's Desert Rose
Kangaroo Paw
Tasmanian Blue Gum

Wreath of Wildflowers Chart 3

KEY FOR WREATH OF WILDFLOWERS:

	DMC cotton	DMC wool		DMC cotton	DMC wool		DMC cotton	DMC wool
· ·	white	ecru	◖ ◖	420	7514	⋈ ⋈	729	7506
⋇ ⋇	209	7709	◣ ◣	433	7514	□ □	734	7676
⫶ ⫶	211	7241	● ●	444	7725	< <	743	7742
↑ ↑	304	7108	╱ ╱	445	7078	I I	746	ecru
╱ ╱	309	7205	6 6	470	7364	+ +	754	7121
◆ ◆	333	7306	V V	471	7362	✕ ✕	782	7783
⊘ ⊘	340	7304	– –	472	7361	R R	783	7783
⌐ ⌐	341	7302	◣ ◣	500	7398	▼ ▼	791	7306
↖ ↖	350	7850	∧ ∧	504	7333	✖ ✖	815	7110
⌐ ⌐	352	7851	✳ ✳	666	7849	✕ ✕	816	7208
S S	355	7196	▽ ▽	676	7506	♡ ♡	818	7132

106

Wreath of Wildflowers Chart 4

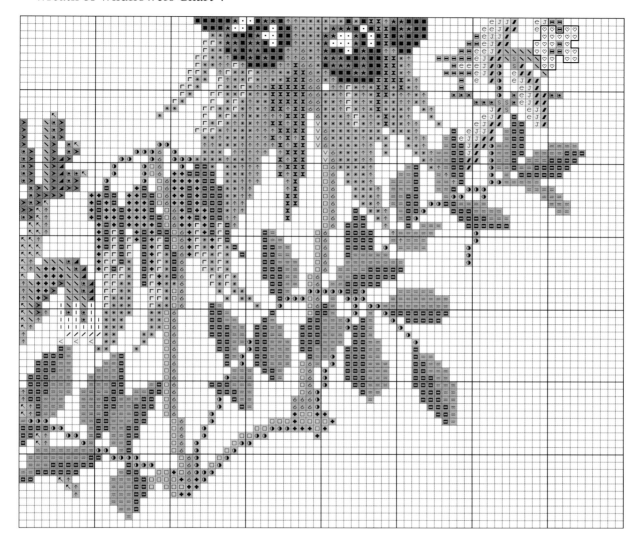

Backstitch around
pale pink petals of
the Common Heath
with one strand of
DMC 899

Stitch Count:
180 across
180 down

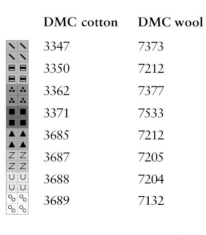

	DMC cotton	DMC wool
▶▶	895	7347
J J	899	7204
★★	902	7115
⊥⊥	935	7391
▫▫	3011	7391
✛✛	3012	7426
══	3052	7392
◣◣	3078	7905
e e	3326	7204
◢◢	3345	7427
◖◖	3346	7376

	DMC cotton	DMC wool
◥◥	3347	7373
▭▭	3350	7212
⁘⁘	3362	7377
■■	3371	7533
▲▲	3685	7212
Z Z	3687	7205
U U	3688	7204
°°°	3689	7132

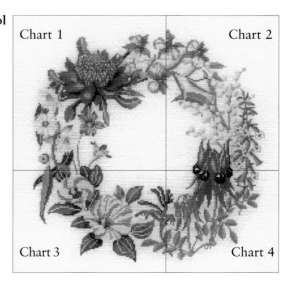

107

Coastal Wildflowers

This embroidery was designed from my original watercolour painting titled 'Wildflowers of Coastal Southern Australia'. The painting was published and widely distributed as a poster by the Botanic Gardens of Adelaide.

The wildflowers were collected over a few years from many areas of the coast and painted individually before I attempted to put them together into the painting. The watercolour painting took about four months to complete. The cross-stitch embroidery took about nine months to design and embroider.

Silver Goodenia

Common and Botanical Names of Coastal Wildflowers:

Sandhill Sword-Sedge *(Lepidosperma concavum)*, Coast Velvet-Bush *(Lasiopetalum discolor)*, Coast Swainson Pea *(Swainsona lessertifolia)*, Native Yam *(Microseris lanceolata)*, Pink Fairies *(Caladenia latifolia)*, Erect Guinea Flower *(Hibbertia riparia)*, Running Postman *(Kennedia prostrata)*, Native Flax *(Linum marginale)*, Old Man's Beard *(Clematis microphylla)*, Australian Trefoil *(Lotus australis)*, Yellow Microcybe *(Microcybe pauciflora)*, Common Sea Heath *(Frankenia pauciflora)*, Common Riceflower *(Pimelea humilis)*, Coast Speedwell *(Veronica hillebrandii)*, Sweet Apple-Berry *(Billardiera cymosa)*, Salmon Correa *(Correa pulchella)*, Silver Goodenia *(Goodenia affinis)*, Stalked Ixiolaena *(Ixiolaena supina)*, Australian Bindweed *(Convolvulus remotus)*, Bower Spinach, *(Tetragonia implexicoma)*, Lavender Daisy *(Olearia ciliata)*, Coast Logania *(Logania crassifolia)*, Eyebright *(Euphrasia collina)*, Lavender Grevillea *(Grevillea lavandulacea)*, Variable Groundsel *(Senecio lautus)*, Billy Button *(Craspedia uniflora)*, Cockies Tongue *(Templetonia retusa)*, White Correa *(Correa alba)*, Dryland Teatree *(Melaleuca lanceolata)*, Love Vine *(Comesperma volubile)*, Spiny Wattle *(Acacia spinescens)*, Coast Twinleaf *(Zygophyllum billardierei)*, Round-Leaved Pigface *(Disphyma crassifolium)*.

Because of the size and density of this design, the flowers in the foreground have been charted separately to the sea and cliffs in the background.

The diagram below shows how the design is divided into sections:
- 6 pages (Charts 1–6) for the **wildflowers** in the **foreground**, and
- 6 pages (Charts 7–12) for the **sea and cliffs** in the **background**.

Stitch Count: 245 across
183 down

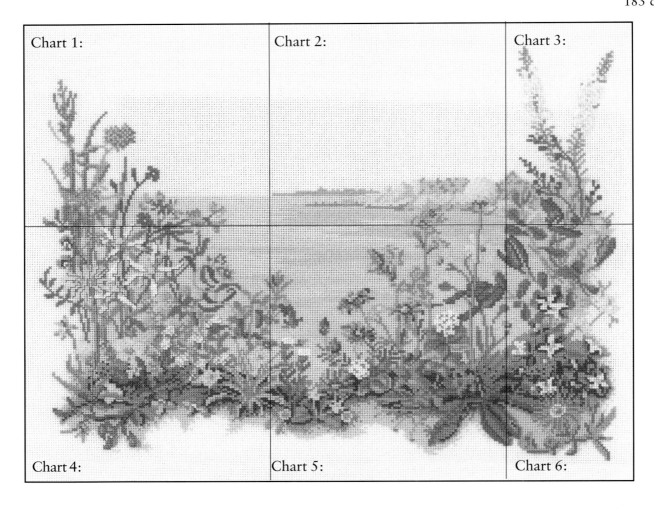

Chart 1:	Chart 2:	Chart 3:
Chart 4:	Chart 5:	Chart 6:

WILDFLOWERS IN FOREGROUND: The **foreground wildflowers** are embroidered first using **two strands** of DMC cotton.

BACKGROUND SEA AND CLIFFS: The **background sea and cliffs** are worked lastly with only **one strand** of DMC cotton.

BACKSTITCHING:

Old Man's Beard—use one strand of DMC 316 around edges of the white petals

Native Yam—use one strand of DMC 434 on petals and on right side of the stem

Billy Button—use one strand of DMC 434 on right side of the stem.

Coastal Wildflowers Chart 1: **WILDFLOWERS**

Running Postman

Coastal Wildflowers Chart 2: **WILDFLOWERS**

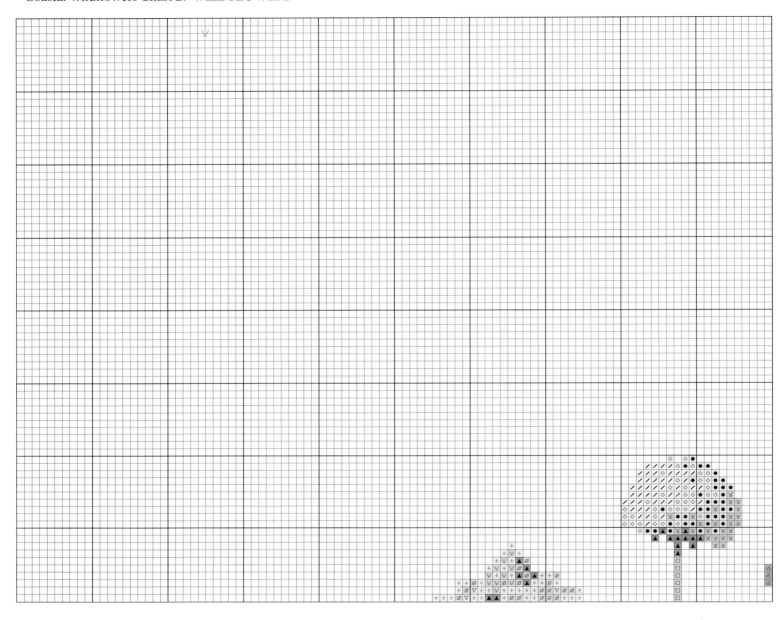

Round-Leaved Pigface

Coastal Wildflowers Chart 3: **WILDFLOWERS**

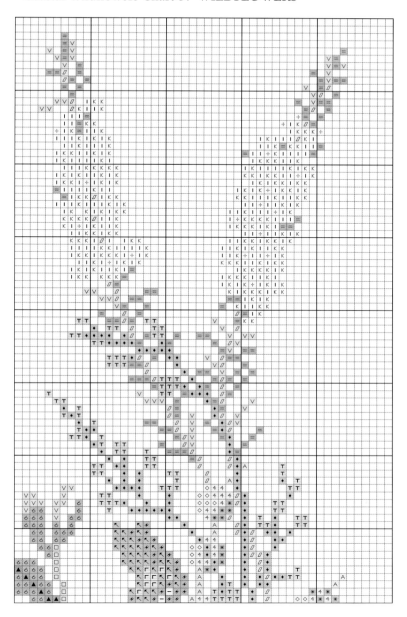

KEY FOR COASTAL WILDFLOWERS

DMC Stranded cotton:

⋅⋅ ⋅⋅	white	⅄ ⅄	729
⋅∶ ⋅∶	211	□ □	734
◇ ◇	307	< <	743
∅ ∅	316	I I	746
◆ ◆	319	3 3	760
I I	320	⊹ ⊹	778
◤ ◤	327	❚ ❚	780
⌐ ⌐	341	R R	783
⚡ ⚡	347	↓ ↓	793
◤ ◤	350	✳ ✳	832
S S	351	■ ■	838
Γ Γ	352	× ×	907
← ←	368	▲ ▲	937
÷ ÷	369	⋰ ⋰	963
▶ ▶	370	F F	987
◣ ◣	433	X X	988
◩ ◩	434	✚ ✚	3012
∩ ∩	436	⊥ ⊥	3013
● ●	444	= =	3052
⁄ ⁄	445	◥ ◥	3078
6 6	470	+ +	3328
V V	471	◢ ◢	3345
− −	472	◖ ◖	3346
◆ ◆	502	＼ ＼	3347
A A	503	✓ ✓	3348
N N	553	Z Z	3687
∘ ∘	554	⊡ ⊡	3688
⫽ ⫽	612	⋈ ⋈	3726
▽ ▽	676	⫽ ⫽	3778
K K	677	⊤ ⊤	3807
⋋ ⋋	726	4 4	3820
2 2	727		

113

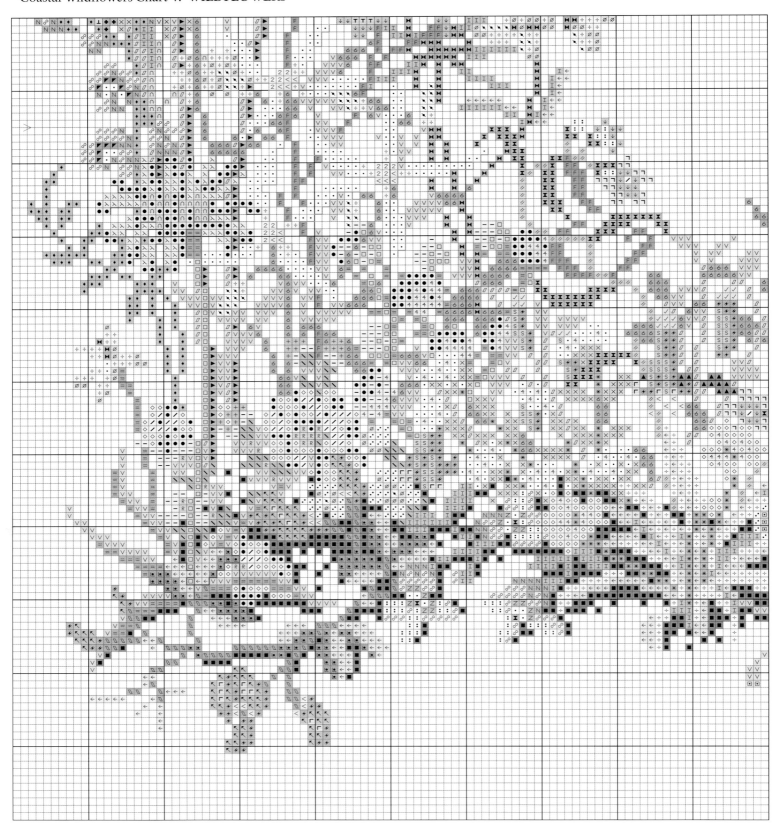

Salmon Correa

Coastal Wildflowers Chart 7: **BACKGROUND SEA & CLIFFS**

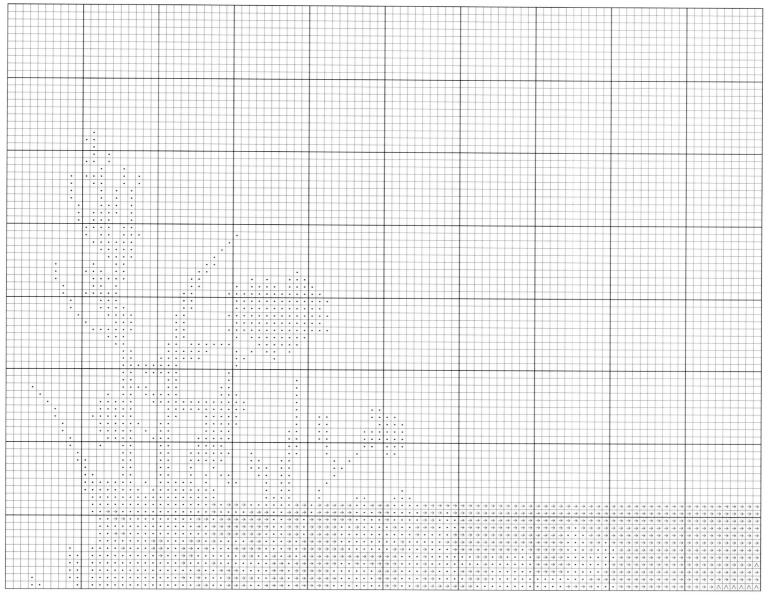

NOTE: For ease of working, the symbols for the background stitches are shown on a colour background, and the symbols for the foreground wildflowers that you have already worked are now shown only as dots on a white background.

Lavender Daisy

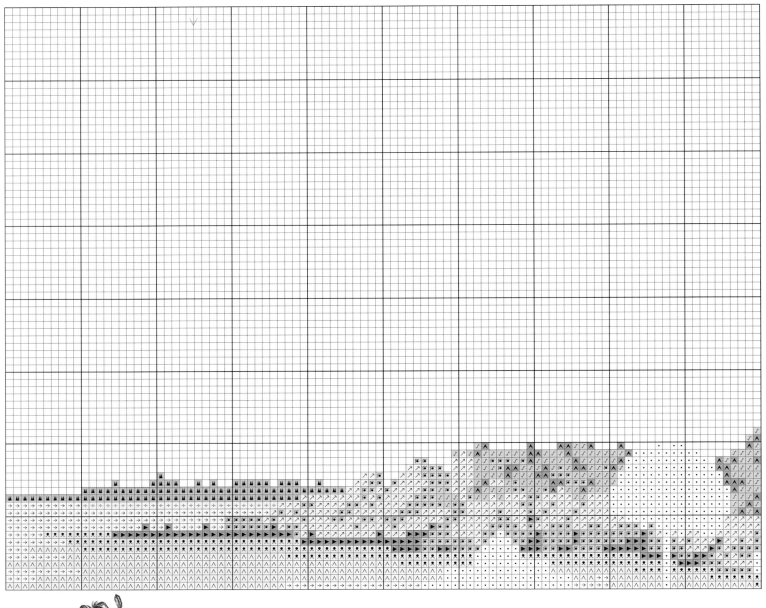

Old Man's Beard (female flower)

Coastal Wildflowers Chart 9: **BACKGROUND SEA & CLIFFS**

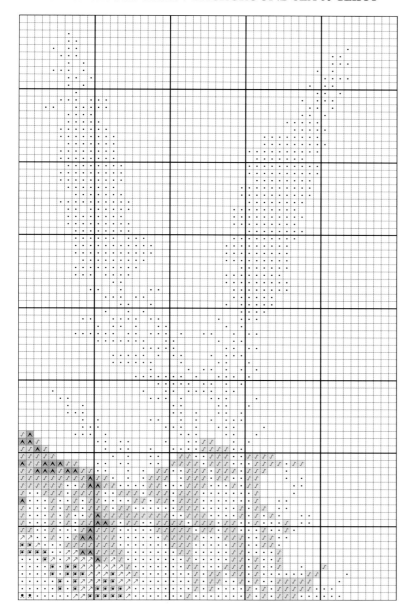

KEY FOR COASTAL BACKGROUND SEA & CLIFFS

DMC stranded cotton:

738	Ground colours	
840		

369	Sea colours
504	
772	
775	
828	
3747	

370	Cliff colours
422	
503	
739	
3347	
3348	

To ensure that the wildflowers stand out against the background, use only one strand of DMC thread for embroidering the foreground, sea and cliffs.

Group of three flowers from Coastal Wildflowers
Daisy, Eyebright and Logania

Coastal Wildflowers Chart 10: **BACKGROUND SEA & CLIFFS**

Coastal Wildflowers Chart 11: **BACKGROUND SEA & CLIFFS**

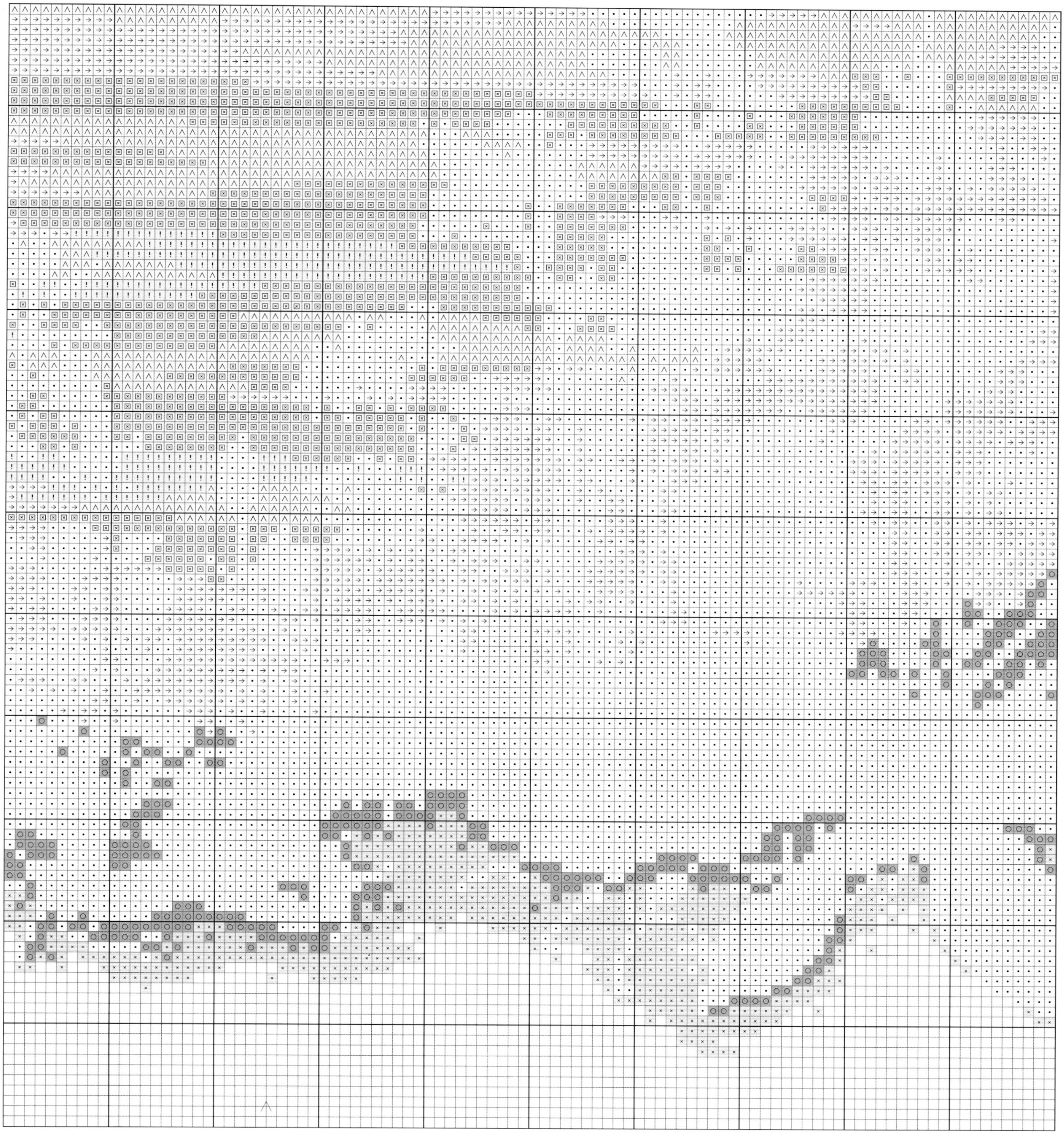

Coastal Wildflowers Chart 12: **BACKGROUND SEA & CLIFFS**

Opposite page:
Yellow Rush-Lily, Satin Everlasting,
Native Flax, Coast Speedwell, Austral
Storks-Bill, Scaly Buttons, Lavender
Daisy, and Bent Goodenia.

Left: Scented Mat-Rush

Native Toadstools

During winter the forest floor comes to life. After good rains the mosses and lichens freshen up giving a startling contrast of green against the dark ground. Fungi begin to grow amongst the damp leaf and bark litter.

I will never forget one magical day when I was looking for toadstools for a painting. I was on a private property consisting of dense stringy-bark forest that had never been cleared. A narrow dirt track led down towards a shallow creek. It was a beautiful day and the sun was shining through the leaves above making everything sparkle. In a few sheltered places fronds of a tiny rock fern were starting to appear, and I saw the tiny leaves of some early orchids. A family of little blue wrens were in the area keeping an eye on me.

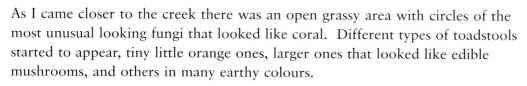

As I came closer to the creek there was an open grassy area with circles of the most unusual looking fungi that looked like coral. Different types of toadstools started to appear, tiny little orange ones, larger ones that looked like edible mushrooms, and others in many earthy colours.

Progressing along the track into thicker scrub the leaf litter also became thicker and I began to find the most incredibly coloured toadstools partly hidden under the dead leaves, or growing on the underside of damp pieces of wood and bark. There were brilliant reds, oranges, purples, yellows and greens, all in startling contrast to the forest floor. It really was a magical day.

Since then I have often gone hunting for toadstools but have never found the same variety and colours growing in such profusion.

The painting on the opposite page shows the red toadstools *(Russula purpureoflava)* and the sweetly scented little sundew *(Drosera whittakeri)*.

Green Toadstools

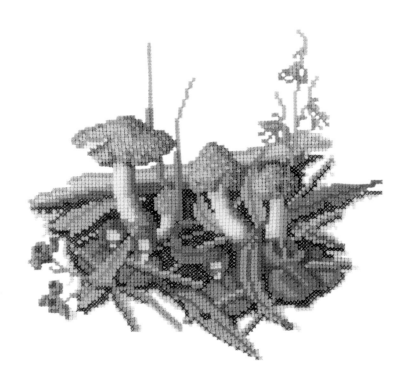

Green Toadstools *(Cortinarius sp)*, are embroidered here nestling amongst leaf litter together with the tiny little **Veined Helmet Orchid** *(Corybas diemenicus)*, and **Winter-Flowering Mosquito Orchid** *(Cyrtostylis robusta)*.

Key for DMC stranded cotton:

W W / W W	355	U U / U U	841
T T / T T	356	= = / = =	842
/ / / / /	420	× × / × ×	907
J J / J J	422	◆ ◆ / ◆ ◆	935
◣ ◣ / ◣ ◣	433	→ → / → →	986
↑ ↑ / ↑ ↑	435	○ ○ / ○ ○	987
▲ ▲ / ▲ ▲	469	I I / I I	989
– – / – –	472	3078	3078
▽ ▽ / ▽ ▽	676	↗ ↗ / ↗ ↗	3328
⚡ ⚡ / ⚡ ⚡	729	● ● / ● ●	3345
▢ ▢ / ▢ ▢	734	◖● ◖● / ◖● ◖●	3346
F F / F F	760	╱ ╱ / ╱ ╱	3347
✳ ✳ / ✳ ✳	838	+ + / + +	3726
K K / K K	839	ᴍ ᴍ / ᴍ ᴍ	3802

Background colours:

· · / · ·	842	(use one strand)
✓ ✓ / ✓ ✓	938	(use one strand)
◼ ◼ / ◼ ◼	3371	(use one strand)

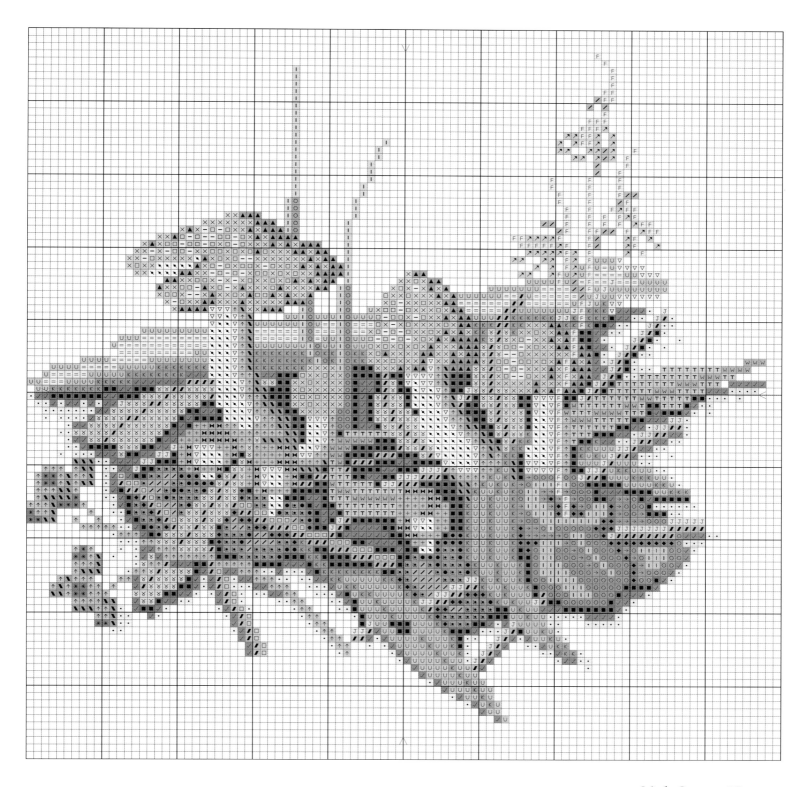

Stitch Count: 98 across
92 down

Purple Toadstools

Purple Toadstools *(Russula mariae)* are embroidered here with **Ivy-leafed Violets** *(Viola hederaceae).*

The Ivy-leafed Violet is a creeping perennial herb that forms large carpets of round green leaves and flowers profusely in damp, sheltered sites in forest and woodland. It is grown widely as a garden plant.

Key for DMC stranded cotton:

white	3021
210	3350
355	3354
356	3609
470	3689
471	3740
554	3823
729	3829
839	3834
840	3835
841	3836
937	

Background colours:

842	(use one strand)
938	(use one strand)
3371	(use one strand)

Stitch Count: 87 across
83 down

Backstitching:

Backstitch around edges of white violet petals as shown using one strand of purple DMC 3835.

Golden Bell Frog

The Golden Bell Frog *(Litoria raniformis)*, is a large muscular frog varying in colour from light green to brown with golden or yellowish-brown markings. It lives amongst the vegetation in rivers, lakes and marshes and is found in Southern and South-Eastern Australia.

Key for DMC stranded cottons:

white	783
ecru	801
310	3021
420	3345
433	3346
436	3347
470	3362
471	209
472	792
500	794
738	

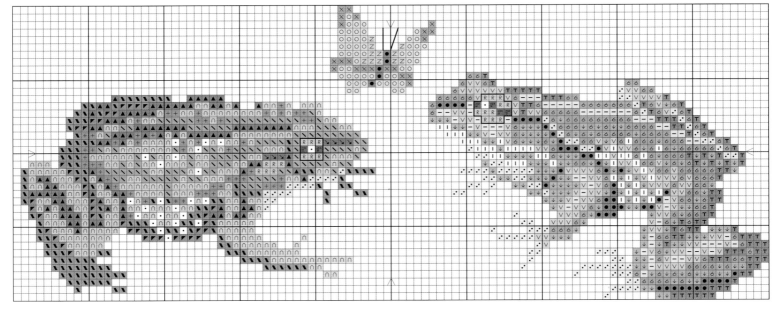

Honey Bees

The painting here shows bees looking for pollen around the Box Mistletoe, *Amyema miquelii,* and blossom of the River Red Gum, *Eucalyptus camaldulensis.*

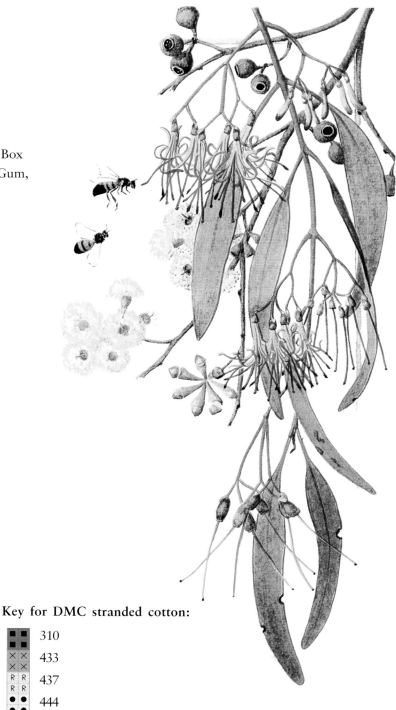

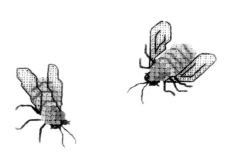

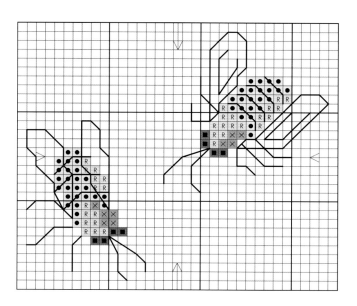

Key for DMC stranded cotton:

■ ■	310
✕ ✕	433
R R	437
● ●	444

Backstitching:

Wings and feelers using one strand of DMC 310

Legs with two strands of DMC 310

Bands on body with two strands of DMC 433

Sugar Glider

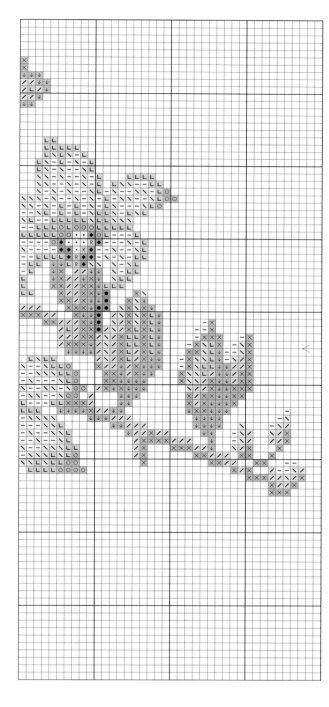

Sugar Glider *(Petaurus breviceps)*
This tiny possum with its large bright eyes and thick soft fur, is one of the most beautiful of the possum family.

By extending the front and back limbs the loose skin along the sides spreads out to form a flying membrane, and they glide about at night in the tree tops. The furry tail acts as a rudder. Tree cavities and hollow limbs provide shelter for their nests.

The Sugar Glider is embroidered here on a flowering branch of a **Lace Bark Tree** *(Brachychiton discolour)*.

Key for DMC stranded cottons:

ı ı	ecru	· ·	727
◆ ◆	221	▽ ▽	758
L L	223	R R	783
\ \	224	● ●	3011
− −	225	× ×	3012
■ ■	310	∕ ∕	3013
⊥ ⊥	356	T T	3021
⌐ ⌐	413	○ ○	3722
▲ ▲	414	⋈ ⋈	3799
↓ ↓	420		
← ←	415/841 (1 strand each)		
Z Z	355/413 (1 strand each)		

Stitch Count: 136 across
86 down

Materials and Instructions

The charts in this book have been embroidered in cross stitch, but can be used in a variety of other ways including tapestry, needlepoint, petitpoint, knitting, beading and rugmaking.

If you are new to cross stitch or have not worked from a chart before, always begin with a small design.

Use the charts as an inspiration for your own creativity. An embroidery can become uniquely yours just by changing thread colours or adding surface embroidery. Changing background fabric colours can also completely change the effect of a design.

Wool colours have been included with three of the larger wildflower designs, 'Wildflower Bouquet 1', 'Wildflower Bouquet 2' and 'Wreath of Wildflowers' to tempt and encourage tapestry embroiderers who have only ever worked from painted or trammed tapestries.

The coloured charts are very easy to work from. Each thread colour is clearly represented by a symbol. No half or quarter stitches have been used and backstitching has been kept to a minimum.

If you find that the chart you wish to embroider is hard to see or too small to work from, enlarge it with the aid of a colour photocopier.

WORKING A DESIGN IN CROSS STITCH

Background fabrics

There are many beautiful fabrics available in a large range of colours. Two popular evenweave materials for cross stitch are linen and aida.

Linen is a natural fabric and so the threads can vary in size giving a slightly uneven look to the finished embroidery. Many embroiderers prefer to use linen. Although cross stitch is usually worked over two threads of linen, beautiful and very dainty results can be achieved by working over only one thread. I have models of the 'Superb Blue Wren' and the 'New Holland Honeyeater' worked in cross stitch using one strand of cotton over one thread of a 32-count linen and they look exquisite.

Aida fabric has a surface of clearly designated squares, producing a more even look to the finished embroidery. The ease of counting stitches on aida makes it a perfect background fabric for the beginner.

A finer background fabric gives more stitches to the inch resulting in a smaller finished embroidery.

Size of background fabric needed

To establish how much background fabric is required for a design you need to know the 'count of the fabric' (number of threads per inch), and the 'stitch count' (number of stitches on the chart) of the design you wish to embroider.

Aida fabric is easy to work out the count as each small square represents one cross stitch, therefore:
- Aida 14 has 14 stitches to the inch
- Aida 16 has 16 stitches to the inch
- Aida 18 has 18 stitches to the inch

Linen count refers to the number of threads per inch. As cross stitch on linen is usually worked over two threads, the thread count needs to be halved, therefore:
- 28 count linen has 14 stitches to the inch
- 30 count linen has 15 stitches to the inch.

The stitch count (number of stitches on the chart) is shown alongside each charted design.

Leave at least 4 inches (10 cm) of fabric on each side of the design to allow for framing, hemming, etc.

Below is an example of how the required size of background fabric was ascertained for the 'Finger Flower', the first design in this book.

- **Stitch Count** for the design is 60 x 129
- background fabric is **linen 30** (15 stitches to the inch)

    Divide 15 into 60 and 129 to find the size of the embroidered area
    = 4 inches x 8.6 inches (10 cms x 22 cms).

    Add 4 inches (10 cms) each side of the design to allow for framing etc.

Total size of background fabric:
    12 inches x 16.6 inches (30 cms x 42 cms).

Threads

There is a wonderful range of embroidery threads available for cross stitch. Although the designs in this book have been worked with DMC Stranded Cotton, other threads, Anchor Stranded Cottons, Au Ver A Soie stranded silks and Finca Stranded Cottons can also be used. Conversion charts for these threads are included with this book.

Au Ver A Soie - Soie d'Alger
These beautiful French stranded silks are a delight to work with and come in a wonderful range of over 660 colours.

Anchor Stranded Cotton
Anchor 100% cotton stranded threads are made in Germany and come in a beautiful range of over 450 colours.

Finca Mouline Stranded Cotton
Finca stranded cottons are produced by Presencia of Spain. Their beautiful range of over 250 colours are 100% colourfast.

Finca Perle is available in over 120 solid colours and 33 shaded colours. This cotton gives a luxurious sheen for fantastic results.

Thread Organiser

A thread organiser is an easy way to keep your threads organised for each design. Cut a piece of card and punch holes down one side. Thread and loop each colour through a different hole and label it with the correct symbol and number.

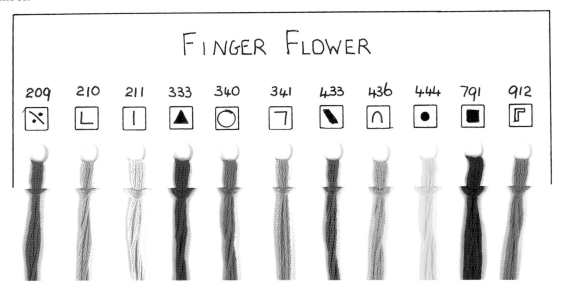

An ideal length of thread is 20 inches (50 cms). Longer threads tend to fray or tangle.

Stitching

Overcast or overlock around the edges of the background fabric to prevent it from fraying. Find the centre of the fabric by folding it in half both ways and then basting along these fold lines with sewing cotton.

Mark the centre of your chart and then begin to stitch from the centre of the fabric and work out. This will ensure that the design will be placed centrally on the fabric.

With a large design it sometimes pays to spend a little extra time and with basting stitches mark the fabric out into blocks of 10 stitches to match your charted design.

Always use a tapestry needle for cross stitch as the end of the needle is blunt and will not pierce the fibres of the fabric. Recommended sizes are 24 or 26.

Never start with a knot in the embroidery thread. Leave a small length of thread at the back of the embroidery and catch it with the first few stitches to hold it secure. To finish, weave the thread ends through the back of four or five stitches and then trim. Be careful not to carry threads across the back of areas that will not be stitched.

Using an embroidery hoop or frame will help keep your background fabric taut so that it does not stretch or distort, and will make stitching easier and more even.

Generally cross stitch is worked over two threads of linen and over the designated squares of aida fabric. Two strands of thread have been used for all the designs in this book unless stated otherwise.

Linen

Aida

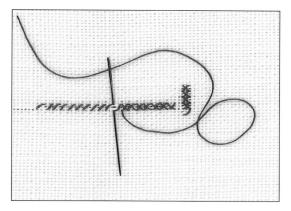
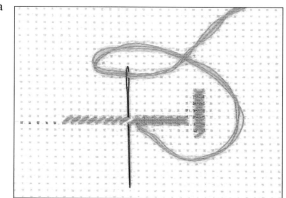

Cross stitch is worked by bringing the needle up in the bottom left of square and taking it down through the top right of square. Repeat this diagonal stitch across the fabric from left to right, and then work back from right to left to complete the cross.

You may stitch from left to right, or from right to left. The only golden rule is to ensure that each stitch on your embroidery is crossed in the same direction.

Backstitch is used to outline parts of a design, and is indicated on the chart by a bold line.

Conversion Chart from DMC Stranded Cotton to –

Anchor Stranded Cotton
Au Ver A Soie Stranded Silk – Soie d'Alger
Finca Mouline Stranded Cotton

DMC		Anchor	Au Ver A Soie	Finca
white	white	2	blanc	1000
ecru	ecru	926	brut	3000
208	lavender vy dk	112	3335	2711
209	lavender dk	110	1342	2699
210	lavender med	108	3334	2687
211	lavender lt	342	3333	2687
221	shell pink vy dk	897	4625	2171
223	shell pink med	895	4622	1981
224	shell pink lt	894	4621	1975
225	shell pink vy lt	892	1011	1969
300	mahogany vy dk	352	4142	7656
304	Christmas red med	47	943	1906
307	lemon	290	534	1222
309	rose deep	29	2934	1661
310	black	403	noir	0007
312	navy blue lt	979	1715	3319
315	antique mauve dk	1019	4645	2123
316	antique mauve med	1017	4633	2110
318	steel grey lt	399	3842	8728
319	pistachio green vy dk	217	3425	4485
320	pistachio green med	215	1834	4478
327	antique violet dk	101	3315	2635
333	violet blue dk	119	1344	-----
334	baby blue med dk	977	1434	3396
335	rose	38	3014	1651
340	violet blue med	118	4912	-----
341	violet blue lt	117	4911	-----
347	salmon dk	1006	942	1490
349	coral dk	13	935	1344
350	coral med	11	934	1485
351	coral	10	933	1485
352	coral lt	9	931	1474
355	terra cotta med dk	1014	2636	1996

DMC		Anchor	Au Ver A Soire	Finca
356	terra cotta med	1013	4612	7813
368	pistachio gn. lt	214	1833	4472
369	pistachio gn.vy lt	1043	1841	4379
370	camel tan dk	855	3715	-----
371	camel tan med	854	3713	-----
372	camel tan lt	853	3713	-----
413	pewter grey dk	400	3445	8785
414	steel grey dk	235	3442	8688
415	pearl grey	398	3441	8767
420	hazelnut brown dk	944	2246	7392
422	hazelnut brown lt	942	3812	7386
433	brown med	358	4516	8075
434	brown lt	371	4236	8072
435	brown vy lt	370	4235	8069
436	tan	369	4234	8069
444	lemon dk	291	631	1227
445	lemon lt	288	2523	1217
469	avocado green	267	245	4823
470	avocado green lt	255	2124	4817
471	avocado green vy lt	254	2123	4812
472	avocado green ultra lt	253	2122	4799
500	blue green vy dk	879	5025	4323
501	blue green dk	877	5024	4231
502	blue green	876	5023	4228
503	blue green med	875	5022	4228
504	blue green lt	1042	5021	4218
517	wedgwood med	162	1446	3494
550	violet vy dk	102	1326	2635
552	violet dk	100	1325	2627
553	violet med	98	3313	2615
554	violet lt	96	3311	2606
610	drab brown vy dk	898	3834	8327
611	drab brown dk	832	4534	8327

DMC		Anchor	Au Ver A Soie	Finca	DMC		Anchor	Au Ver A Soie	Finca
612	drab brown med	831	3833	8320	823	navy blue dk	150	1425	3324
613	drab brown lt	830	3832	8310	825	blue dk	162	1446	3319
640	beige grey med dk	393	3444	8327	826	blue med	161	1445	3229
666	Christmas red brt	46	936	1163	827	blue vy lt	159	1442	3219
676	old gold lt	891	2532	7139	828	blue ultra vy lt	9159	1441	3802
677	old gold vy lt	956	2231	1134	832	antique gold med lt	907	2235	7057
722	pumpkin spice vy lt	323	644	7726	838	beige brown vy dk	381	4136	8171
725	topaz	305	623	1010	839	beige brown dk	1050	3436	8159
726	topaz lt	295	624	1010	840	beige brown med	903	3345	8157
727	topaz vy lt	293	625	1220	841	beige brown lt	388	3432	8145
729	old gold med	890	2535	7155	842	beige brown vy lt	387	3431	8140
734	olive green lt	279	2211	4799	890	pistachio grn ultra dk	1044	1836	4323
738	tan vy lt	366	2611	8060	895	Christmas green dk	218	1845	4485
739	tan ultra vy lt	276	4241	4000	898	coffee brown vy dk	380	4123	8080
741	tangerine med	304	621	1152	899	rose med	26	3013	1651
742	tangerine lt	303	622	1232	902	garnet vy dk	897	2926	2171
743	yellow med	302	522	1062	906	parrot green med	256	244	4730
745	yellow lt pale	301	2531	1134	907	parrot green lt	255	244	4723
746	off white	275	2541	1211	912	emerald green lt	209	213	4396
754	peach flesh lt	1012	2912	1301	919	red copper	340	611	7580
758	terra cotta lt	882	4611	7806	927	grey green med	848	1742	3721
760	salmon	1022	2943	1889	928	grey green lt	274	1731	3721
761	salmon lt	1021	2942	1975	930	antique blue dk	1035	1714	3151
762	pearl grey vy lt	234	4140	8683	931	antique blue med	1034	1713	3139
772	celery green lt	259	2111	4379	932	antique blue lt	1033	1712	3139
775	baby blue lt	975	1711	3299	935	avocado green vy dk	862	3726	4565
776	pink med	24	2941	1645	937	avocado green med	861	3723	4823
778	antique mauve lt	1016	4631	2098	939	navy blue vy dk	127	161	3327
780	topaz vy dk	310	2516	8072	963	dusty rose vy lt	23	2941	1724
782	topaz med	308	2515	1072	975	golden brown dk	349	2616	7740
783	Christmas gold	307	2514	1068	976	golden brown med	1001	2546	7731
791	cornflower blue vy dk	178	4916	3411	977	golden brown lt	1002	2614	7726
792	cornflower blue dk	177	4914	3405	986	forest green vy dk	246	2116	4906
793	cornflower blue med	176	4912	3400	987	forest green dk	244	2115	4561
794	cornflower blue lt	175	4911	3396	988	forest green med	243	234	4885
801	coffee brown dk	359	4122	8080	989	forest green	241	233	4885
809	delft	130	1434	3396	3011	khaki green dk	845	3724	5236
813	blue lt	1038	1443	3223	3012	khaki green med	843	3734	5229
814	garnet dk	45	946	1915	3013	khaki green lt	842	3721	5224
815	garnet med	44	944	1915	3021	brown grey dk	905	3836	8589
816	garnet	43	945	1667	3022	brown grey med	8581	3424	8574
818	baby pink	48	1012	1721	3023	brown grey vy lt	900	3422	8567

DMC		Anchor	Au Ver A Soie	Finca	DMC		Anchor	Au Ver A Soie	Finca
3032	mocha brown med	392	4533	8320	3768	grey green dk	779	1745	3739
3041	antique violet med	872	5113	8620	3778	terra cotta med dk	1013	923	7813
3042	antique violet lt	870	5112	8605	3781	mocha brown dk	905	3435	8327
3045	yellow beige dk	888	2243	7392	3787	brown grey med dk	273	3443	8492
3046	yellow beige med	887	2242	7386	3799	pewter grey vy dk	236	3845	8756
3051	grey green dk	861	3716	5156	3801	Christmas red lt	35	1025	-----
3052	grey green med	859	3714	5151	3802	antique mauve vy dk	897	4636	2123
3053	grey green	858	3423	5140	3803	mauve dk	69	3026	2246
3078	golden yellow vy lt	292	533	1214	3807	cornflower blue	122	4912	3400
3325	baby blue med lt	976	4921	3305	3816	sea green	208	1823	4350
3326	rose lt	25	3012	1729	3819	moss green	278	243	-----
3328	salmon med dk	1024	2916	1895	3820	harvest gold dk	306	2525	1040
3345	hunter green dk	268	2126	4565	3821	harvest gold med	305	2512	1010
3346	hunter green	266	2125	4561	3823	yellow pale vy lt	386	2542	7128
3347	hunter green med	265	2124	4885	3826	golden brown m dk	1049	4214	7740
3348	yellow green lt	264	2113	4550	3827	golden brown vy lt	311	641	7720
3350	antique rose dk	77	3025	2165	3829	old gold vy dk	901	2245	7155
3354	antique rose lt	74	3011	1645	3834	mulberry	100	4646	2635
3362	antique green dk	861	1843	5156	3835	mulberry med	98	1314	2615
3371	black brown	382	4146	8083	3836	mulberry lt	96	1313	2606
3609	orchid vy lt	85	1311	2394					
3685	mauve vy dk	1028	3026	2246					
3687	mauve	76	3024	2240					
3688	mauve med	75	3021	2232					
3689	mauve lt	73	1041	2147					
3712	salmon med	1023	2915	1889					
3716	dusty rose lt	25	3011	1645					
3721	shell pink dk	896	4624	1996					
3722	shell pink med dk	1027	4623	1984					
3726	antique mauve m dk	1018	4644	2110					
3733	antique rose med lt	75	3022	2232					
3740	antique violet dk	873	5114	8620					
3743	antique violet vy lt	869	3331	8599					
3746	violet blue med dk	1030	1343	-----					
3747	violet blue vy lt	117	1711	-----					
3755	baby blue med	976	4922	3312					

NOTE:

The colours in the conversion chart above have been chosen to represent as closely as possible the colours in my paintings and the DMC thread colours used in the embroideries.